Writers Workshop of Horror

"A veritable treasure trove of information for aspiring writers—straight from the mouths of today's top horror scribes!"

— *Rue Morgue Magazine*

"Packing more knowledge and sound advice than four years' worth of college courses . . . It's focused on the root of your evil, the writing itself."

— *Fangoria Magazine*

"Entertaining, informative, and also plain old fun, this book will not only make you want to write more, it will give you the tools to write better. This should be mandatory reading in creative writing classes."

— *Horror World*

Writers Workshop of Horror

Editor Michael Knost

WOODLAND PRESS, LLC
USA

ALSO BY
WOODLAND PRESS
And Edited by Michael Knost

Legends of the Mountain State

Ghostly Tales from the State of West Virginia

Legends of the Mountain State 2

More Ghostly Tales from the State of West Virginia

Legends of the Mountain State 3

More Ghostly Tales from the State of West Virginia

Appalachian Holiday Hauntings

ISBN 978-0-9824939-1-5

SAN: 254-9999

Table of Contents

Introduction

Michael Knost

I DIDN'T HAVE A MENTOR when I started writing. In fact, living in southern West Virginia, I didn't know a single soul who remotely came close to being a writer. I knew I was making novice mistakes, but I had no way of differentiating what was good and what was bad. Don't get me wrong, I had worked in radio for twenty years so I knew how to communicate, and I felt I was a decent storyteller. But I was smart enough to know I was getting rejection letters for a reason.

I eventually discovered a few online critique groups, but quickly realized most participants offered amateur and / or ill-informed advice. These folks—most of whom have never published—were offering suggestions about a craft they knew nothing about. This is why you should always know your fellow critiquers. And keep in mind these folks can only offer an opinion.

It wasn't until I attended a few nationally recognized workshops and boot camps that I began recognizing my writing problems. Not only did I benefit from the critiques and lessons, I also found the networking to be equally valuable. Meeting other writers in the same boat (and level) was priceless. Long after the workshops, we continued critiquing one another's works.

I wish I could have read *Writers Workshop of Horror* during my first year in the craft. I'm sure I could have developed faster, improving my work by leaps and bounds with its advice. This is why this project is so important to me. If you are a beginner, I hope you master the basics. If you've been writing for a while, I hope you learn a few new tricks.

I would like to point out that I have taken a slightly different approach to editing this project. I wanted to make sure each article or interview retained its individuality and author style. I was not attempting to make this a uniformed whole . . . I merely wanted it to be a diverse collection of advice from multiple viewpoints and tone. Because of this, you will find varying structures and styles that solely belong to each contributing author. This means Ramsey Campbell's piece remains untouched when it comes to his unique style and structure. The same goes for Joe R. Lansdale, Brian Keene, and every other contributor.

My involvement was merely that of a contractor overseeing the building of a beautiful home, as contractors hire the best individuals according to his or her needs. The contractor doesn't hire an individual who excels in drywall to wire the house . . . He or she hires the best electrician. Then he or she hires the drywall specialist to do the drywalling. In the same vein, I invited some of the best in the business to deliver pieces on specific craft elements as it pertains to the dark fiction genres.

This book is meant to focus solely on honing the craft of writing. You won't find anything in these pages on marketing, promotions, or submission tips. That's another book for another time. What you will find is solid advice—from professionals of every publishing level—on how to improve your writing.

Although this project is centered on writing horror and/or dark fiction, the principles and advice will transcend all genres and all forms of writing. It doesn't matter if you write romance, science fiction, western, mysteries, fantasy, or memoirs, you will benefit from the information, ultimately improving your craft by bringing polished elements of horror, fear, anxiety, or dread to your work when needed.

I salute you for your desire to improve your work . . . *Here's to creating better nightmares.*

Order additional copies of *Writers Workshop of Horror* directly at:
www.writersworkshopofhorror.com

Special thanks to artist Marcelo Duarte for allowing Woodland Press to use the blood spatter art for the cover.

CHAPTER 1

Elizabeth Massie

Once Upon a Scary Time: Creating Effective Beginnings

ELIZABETH MASSIE is a two-time Bram Stoker Award-winning author whose books include *Sineater, Wire Mesh Mothers, Welcome Back to the Night, Shadow Dreams, Homeplace,* and many others. Her short fiction has appeared in numerous magazines and anthologies such as *Outsiders, Hottest Blood, Years Best Fantasy* and *Horror 4, Best New Horror* 2 and 17, *Exotic Gothic 2,* and *The Mammoth Book of Vampire Stories by Women.* Upcoming works for 2009 include the novel *DD Murphry, Secret Policeman* (co-authored with Alan M. Clark) and a comic book featuring The Phantom and his twin sister, Julie. In addition to writing, Beth is the creator of the *Skeeryvilletown* cartoon universe. She shares life and abode in the Shenandoah Valley of Virginia with illustrator Cortney Skinner. Her website is www.elizabethmassie.com, and items featuring her *Skeeryvilletown* cartoon creatures are available at http://www.cafepress.com/skeeryvilletown.

"When he opened the glove compartment he expected to find the registration papers the policeman had just requested, not a shriveled, blackened hand sawed off at the wrist."

Okay, now that I have your attention, let's talk about writing effective or intriguing openings to horror stories or novels.

What makes you stop along the street and stare? Probably not the ordinary-looking people hurrying here and there on their ways to work or the gym. Probably not the stoplight, or the newspaper box, or the wheeled plastic garbage bin waiting for the city collection truck to come by and claim its contents.

But what if one of the people in that ordinary, hurrying herd on the street has only one eye in the middle of her head? What if the stoplight began to flash out a repeated auditory warning message—"There is only an hour left!"—as it continued to flick back and forth from green to yellow to red? What if the front page of the newspaper in the box read, "Obama Decides to Step Down—Encourages All to Vote Palin For President!" What if you witnessed several dark red, slithering, foot-long, slug-like creatures crawling up and out of the garbage bin but no one else could see them?

Now all those circumstances would very likely cause you to stop and stare. And then wonder. And then fear. All within a matter of seconds, probably. This is how you need to think about the openings of your horror stories or novels. Some of the most effective horror stories are set in initially recognizable times and places, with initially recognizable people. But then it all gets turned on its head.

A good story connects to the reader on both an emotional and intellectual level. In the case of horror, the emotional and intellectual level is somewhere in the dark recesses of the heart and mind. Your opening is the first and very possibly last opportunity to make this connection. Because if you don't grab the reader by the heart or the mind and even the gut, then he or she will very likely move on to another story. Unless it's your friend reading your story and he or she has already promised to let you know what they think about the story when they've finished reading. And as you well know, friends aren't always as forthcoming about shortcomings as they should be.

Your first sentence or at least your first paragraph should tease the reader. An effective opening is sometimes called a "hook." You read it, you feel that sharp metal barb catch in your mind or heart or gut, and you are compelled to move deeper into the story, to read more and find out what will happen next. And that's a key right there—what will *happen* next. Because if something doesn't happen right off the bat, or if the reader doesn't feel something impending, then there can't be a "happens next." And your reader will toss your story or novel down and go off to get a beer and watch "Speeders" or "Cash Cab."

I know I'm going to sound like a grumpy old writer with this comment, but you can't live for a period of time as an observant person and not make comparisons to the way things once were and the way they are now. That's not a judgment call; it's fact. And here's something all writers of the early 21st century need to know—most people (readers and editors alike) want instant gratification. They can't wait, like kids on Christmas Eve or in line to ride Space Mountain in Disney World. I could go into a tirade against the short attention-span influences of MTV editing, the countless channels on television, the "watch what you want to watch when you want to watch it" capabilities of Tivo, fast food restaurants, books that "teach" kids to read by talking to them when the kids run special pens across the words, teens being able to communicate with friends at any given moment in time thus disallowing them the chance to learn the beauty of solitude, but I won't. Okay, maybe I just kinda did. But regardless, this is all part of our current culture. Granted, being able to delay gratification is an excellent skill to which we should all aspire. But as horror fiction writers our role is not to teach readers how to delay their gratification. Our role is to throw out that hook, reel in the readers, and subject them to the mental and emotional ups and downs that are part of the ride.

Now, an opening to a horror story or novel does not have to be heart pounding. It can be slow and enticing and disturbing, as long as it satisfies the need for the reader to be teased, compelled, or connected. For example, the opening line in my novel *Homeplace* (Berkley Books, 2007, written as "Beth Massie") reads simply, "They waited until twilight to open the well." Not only did I choose those words carefully but I also set it apart as a single line, opening paragraph. The reader doesn't yet know who "they" are, but the reader immediately knows several things from this single sentence—there is a well, it is closed or covered up, there are people curious as to what is in the well, and for some reason they want to or have to wait until it gets dark to open it. A lot is planted in the readers mind in that one sentence, making them wonder, *what will happen next?*

So what are some ways to create an effective, hooky, compelling, mind/heart/gut-grabbing opening? Here are some suggested techniques to consider.

Start in the middle of a scene.

In my short story, "Fixtures of Matchstick Men and Joo" (*Revelations,* Harper Prism, 1997), I begin with:

> "Gary scrambled around the wounded guy and dropped behind a rusted trash barrel on the street corner. The blood on his hands belonged to an injured man, to a woman, and to himself; Gary had tried to help the wounded guy, to pull him out of the way of the projectiles and the billowing clouds of gas, but he had been knocked unconscious and was too heavy to pull. And as Gary had stood to look for help, to raise his arms amid the madness to wave for someone, something to come to their aid, a screaming goon lashed out with his club and split the skin of his palms and broke the tips of two fingers."

This story is a disturbing psychological horror tale that deals with innocence, hope, and the abuse of power. The opening is—so I've been told by readers—startling and unsettling. And it takes place smack dab in the middle of a scene. Clearly the main character, Gary, is in immediate, possibly mortal, danger. The reader knows very little about this character, nor does he or she have a clear idea of where or when this is taking place, but the tension hits the ground running. Gary is hurt. Others are hurt. He tried to help someone else but failed. There are projectiles and clouds of gas and a screaming goon with a club. What place is this? Who is Gary and why is he there? Why have things become so violent? Why does Gary want to help save the unconscious man? The reader doesn't know. And so the reader, hopefully, wants to read on to find out what is going on here.

Include a peculiar twist or unexpected detail to make your reader wonder.

In my story, "Pinkie" (*A Little Magenta Book of Mean Stories*, Borderlands Press, 2005; *Best New Horror 17*, Carroll & Graf, 2006), I begin with:

> Come September, Rennie didn't like Pinkie so much anymore. The friendship had been going sour throughout the summer, and when it was time to go to the State Fair, Rennie wasn't sure he even wanted to bother. Who wanted to ride two hours to Richmond with a hulking, bristly pig that stared at you, drooled on the passenger's seat, and popped his little red stick in and out, in and out, like an angry and bald prairie dog?

Okay, maybe it's not unusual for farmers to have some sort of affection for some of their farm animals. I mean pigs, how cute are they? Didn't you watch "Babe"? But in this case, I created a strange twist. Rennie, clearly the pig's owner, doesn't like the pig much anymore. For some reason their "friendship" has been going sour over the summer. Now, there is a difference between having affection for a farm animal and calling the relationship a "friendship." It was my intention that the reader would wonder about that twist—a friendship between an ugly, hulking, drooling, exhibitionist pig and Rennie, the pig's owner, a friendship that is now on the fritz. Creepy, don't you think? I thought so, too.

Put your reader immediately into the psychological mindset of your character with a musing of some sort, but make sure the musing is about something strange, dark, or unsettling.

My short story "Pit Boy" (*Outsiders*, ROC, 2005) is told in first person, and the tale opens with the main character considering his surroundings:

> Erik grunted in the shadows to my right, cussed, and then grunted again. I couldn't see his face, only the rough outline of his hunched-up body. I didn't care that I couldn't really see him. He was an asshole, and ugly, too, with screwed-up buckteeth and a nose that looked like an old potato gone bad. Erik didn't like to shoot the bull like the rest of us did, and most of the time just grunted or cussed or talked to hisself. Occasionally he spit big old wet loogies in my direction. He blamed me for everything wrong in his life, but to hell with it, it wasn't my fault.

Immediately the reader knows the situation in which the main character and Erik find themselves is twisted somehow. A reader will wonder, "Why is it dark?" "Why is Erik cussing and grunting?" "Why doesn't Erik like to shoot the bull?" "Who are 'the rest of us'?" "What is wrong with Erik's life and why does he blame the main character?"

If opening your story with a setting, make sure the setting is "lousy with potential." In other words, the setting should be so rich, so tangible, and unsettling that your reader will be champing at the bit to find out "who goes there?"

This one is harder to pull off, but it can be done. I took the chance with this when writing the opening scene for my novel *Wire Mesh Mothers* (Leisure, 2001):

> Orphaned cotton bits, blown loose from the butchered fields of December, scattered themselves across the chipped blacktop of the county roads outside the small town of Pippins, Virginia. They danced their ice dance, dodging automobile tires, winding up for the most part dead along the roadsides and wrapped like suicidal ghosts about the bases of mailbox posts. Sometimes kids played in the harvested fields, picking the remnant fiber, stuffing it down the fronts of their shirts to make big boobs like Miss Carole, the Sunday School teacher down at the Riverside Church of Christ of Nazareth, or making lightweight snowmen by rolling pieces together into big balls and then pinning the pieces together with thistle thorns. It didn't snow much in Pippins, and real snowmen were hard to come by in the winter.

Not a single main character is introduced in this opening paragraph. There is no terror or clearly impending doom. But there is a sense of foreboding; I chose to use words such as "butchered" and "suicidal" and "ghosts" in order to give the setting to mood I was looking for. Even though there isn't one specific action going on here, I offer to the reader the stark, cold harshness of this clearly southern, clearly rural area, and the boredom with which its children go out to play with scattered bits of cotton fluff and the thorns they find in the fields. It's like a festering boil ready to burst, and so the reader is left thinking, "who goes there?" "What will happen next?"

Now that we've considered some things you can do to create enticing openings, here are a few no-nos to avoid when writing the opening to your horror story.

1. - Don't feel the need to flesh out your characters on page one, to reveal everything about him or her for fear the reader won't understand or relate to your character. Nothing worse than having to wade through her red silky hair, brilliant blue eyes, pouting lips (damn, but I hate pouting lips), quirky eyeglasses, and black Goth boots and chains before the female protagonist (or antagonist) says or does a single thing. Well, okay, there are surely worse things but still. Remember, you teach your readers about your characters three ways—by what they say, what they think, and what they do. And these things should come naturally in the flow of the story, not from some resume or characteristic checklist you plunk down early on.

2. - Don't leave out important details in your opening. Give the readers enough to feel they are there; give them some fascinating bits to grasp on to or they might slip away from you.

3. - Don't throw in so many details that the pacing of your opening bogs down. Too many adjectives and adverbs in an opening—or elsewhere—comes across as desperate. Choose such descriptions carefully and sparingly.

4. - And very importantly, don't feel like your opening has to be perfect before you allow yourself to write the rest of the story. Just write

the story. Then you can go back later and, with a fresh eye, revisit your opening. Nothing's done until it's done, and nobody needs to read your work until you're ready for them to do so.

One last bit of advice. Take time to revisit your favorite short horror stories and novels by other writers. Really look at what the writer did on the first page, within the first paragraph, or even with the first sentence. Each opening will all be different, of course. Some will begin with dialogue, or action, or a musing, or a setting. Some introduce a disturbed mind talking to itself. Some drop you right into the middle of a zombie attack. Some board you up in a dark cellar with the smell of corpses all around you. But what they will all have in common is that ability to connect to something inside you, to grab your heart and mind and gut and imaginations, and steer you in the right direction, which is on down into the bowels of the rest of the story.

CHAPTER 2

Michael Laimo

Middles: The Meat of the Matter

MICHAEL LAIMO has written the novels *Fires Rising, Dead Souls, Atmosphere, Deep In The Darkness,* and *The Demonologist,* all of which were published in paperback by Leisure Books. He has also had a dark S/F-Suspense novel, *Sleepwalker,* published in Limited Edition hardcover by Delirium Books. He's also written and published over 100 short stories. Michael can be contacted through his website at www.laimo.com, or through www.mspace.com/michaellaimo. Additional information can be found at www.dorchesterpub.com, and www.myspace.com/anxiety movie.

As connoisseurs of horror fiction, we may consider each novel we read as a meal to consume, one divided into courses: appetizer (set-up), main dish (middle), and dessert (conclusion). Even though every course is as satisfying as the next, only one can be the *most* critical element. This is the middle.

The middle section of a horror novel is your main course: the most fulfilling part of your novel. The meat of the matter. It's where everything *happens,* and where all the drama takes place. Here the set-up matures into action, ultimately evolving to the writer's target of a satisfying conclusion.

As vital as it is in a horror novel to create a beginning that hooks your reader, writing the perfect middle is more challenging an undertaking, as the reader not only wants to be hooked, but gutted and filleted too. Your goal as a writer is to draw an emotional response from the reader, whether it's to quietly elicit cold sweat and goose bumps from your reader, or to gross them out with vivid extremes. Regardless, it all must be accomplished effectively, utilizing a variety of emotions. And this all happens in the middle.

In short, the middle of your book is where you'll stand or fall… where your story will either win or lose the reader. And as a writer of horror, you definitely don't want to let a reader down.

See, readers of horror fiction are picky. They have no problem giving a novel a shot, but are quick to abandon it if it doesn't keep them on edge. I call this the hundred-page rule—if you haven't won the reader over in a hundred pages, then you'll need to go back to the drawing board (or in this case, your middle), and find out what you did wrong.

If the main course tastes bad, it's going in the garbage.

In the set-up, or beginning of your book, you've established character, setting, and key background information. You've set the stage for the roller coaster ride that's about to ensue. Hopefully by page fifty, you'll have introduced a sympathetic and interesting protagonist with a problem, in a setting that's appealing and atmospheric, all written in a unique tone—your voice. The beginning also clues in the reader as to the future context of the story—how the character might deal with their problem.

It's a taste of what's to come. An appetizer.

The middle is your story's meat and potatoes—the beating heart that keeps the blood flowing (and the pages turning). By now the protagonist has already learned about their problem and will face it with an aim to do something about it. But they *will not* succeed in trying. Most of the time when a character faces their demons for the first time, they run away and hide. This gives them time to think over the situation and lay out a plan on what to do. There are plenty of pages later on to have them actually attempt to take control of the situation. After all, we wouldn't have a middle at all if the main character actually faces their demons and kills them on the first try, right? So it's imperative to have your protagonist *fail* in their first attempt to solve their problem. In fact, it's equally important he makes matters worse in the process.

This leads to one of the more crucial aspects of a successful middle: foreshadowing. At the onset of your middle, where your protagonist begins to face his- or her demons for the first time (and ultimately does little to stop them), you must foreshadow what's about to happen—let readers in on the unforeseen failure. In my novel *Deep in the Darkness,* Dr. Michael Cayle moves his family from New York City to their new home in Ashborough, New Hampshire. As they acclimate themselves to the friendly, small-town environment, Michael is faced with his first demon in the form of an elderly neighbor who brings him up into the surrounding woodland to show him what appears to be an ancient sacrificial altar made of stone. Despite some minor forecasts early on, it's here readers are delivered their first 'blow to the gut', so to speak, telling them there's something wrong here in small town New Hampshire, something the protagonist didn't know about. A sacrificial altar? It only stands to reason that the pages will keep turning until someone (or something) gets killed on it.

But effective foreshadowing only goes a short way if you don't follow it up with something else—an unrelated scene that keeps the action alive. If Michael Cayle were to fall back at this point into the everyday humdrum of small town life in New Hampshire, it would be a chore for readers (and unfair to them as well) to wallow through a series of non-events before getting to the sacrifice. So we need the protagonist's problems to *multiply.*

As mentioned, it's important for the main character's problems to grow worse as they attempt to make them better. This enables the writer to tack on some twists and turns into the plot that not only makes the story more interesting, but breathes life into the action. In my novel *Dead Souls,* Benjamin Conroy, a Christian Minister, is convinced that he has unveiled a code in the bible that proves Jesus Christ's rise from the dead was due to a lifelong study of Egyptian black magic. Benjamin feels that if he applies these same rituals to his family, he will *save* their souls from damnation. What readers discover, ultimately, is that Benjamin is actually damning their souls. He is making matters worse. As events spiral downward for Benjamin, he continues to elicit what he believes is the benevolent spirit Osiris, when in fact he is summoning an evil spirit in disguise. The more he attempts to make things better, the worse things become.

By making things worse in the middle, you can now build upon the mounting tension with scenes of action. In *Dead Souls*, as Benjamin continues to unwittingly wreak havoc for himself and his family, we are now able to follow the travails of each and every family member: the wife, the son, the daughter, all of whom are all horribly affected by Benjamin's futile (and unsuccessful) efforts to bring them salvation. It's here I was really able to let my imagination run wild. I knew as I was writing these ensuing scenes, that I could really explore any horrific territory I wished, as long as it fit the context of my story.

When you reach the stage in the middle where the problem is faced, dealt with, and made worse, then you've leaped a major hurdle.

It's *here* all the fun stuff starts, where the momentum really takes off. Where that first climb on the roller coaster is now behind us, and momentum takes over. The horrors have been unleashed. Bad things are happening all over. Now you can let loose with your imagination (as I did with the family in *Dead Souls*) and your descriptive passages. This is the part of the novel that really ignites interest in the horror reader—they really want to see the horrors taking place. So give them your best shot!

But remember this: your darkness only works if there's a light to test it. This light is your protagonist. The harder the protagonist works against the darkness—and make certain it is all of his own resourcefulness—the more readers will root for him and keep the pages turning well into the night. The best way to continue building your protagonist's development is to keep him busy in the center of the action—keep him facing those problems!

Through it all, your protagonist *must* have something dear and personal in jeopardy. Whether it be his own life or the lives of his loved ones, there has to be something more than just his personal ideals at stake. A theme many horror novels explore is the undying bond of love between family members, and how the protection of a child or spouse many times overrides that of one's personal salvation. An interesting protagonist will put his own life in the firing line in order to protect the lives of his family. Michael Cayle did it in *Deep in the Darkness*, and Bev Mathers did it in my novel *The Demonologist*.

As well, your protagonist must be built up in a way that helps increase the suspense factor in your story. Your main character is at the center of much of the action and is being used to forward the plot line. This much is obvious. But he also must be *enhanced* through his emotional response of the terrifying experience. A character's inner development will most assuredly aid in the nail-biting aspects of your story. Here's an excerpt from my novel *Dead Souls*, where my protagonist hears noises coming from his father's bedroom:

> Panic began to flourish in his body, hard ripples of gooseflesh invading his back, angry tingles marching down his spine. He closed his eyes and took a huge breath, trying to beat back the panic. He imagined his body as a plastic mannequin, naked and vulnerable in some dusty stockroom, unable to make any type of showing. Only his mind seemed to be working now, and it told him as he bit a knuckle that he needed to get into the room.

Here the character's emotional response helps further the plot and adds suspense to the scene. The reader feels the character's fear as he looks over his shoulder, anxiously awaiting the horrors that prowl on the other side of the door.

Another critical element to your middle is the amount of time your protagonist has to defeat his demons. Like a ticking bomb, if there's a threat of too much time lapsing, the demons may grow stronger. So tighten your time frame, and put the pressure on your protagonist to conquer his demons quickly, before it's too late. In every horror novel lurks a witching hour, where someone is bound to perish should the protagonist not get his job done in time. Yours should too.

It also stands to reason that most successful horror novels contain characters that are just like you and I. Everymen and women caught in horrible situations against all odds. We live vicariously through their eyes—we enjoy the lighter side of fear a successful horror novel brings, especially if we readers can see ourselves in the shoes of the protagonist. A horror novel with a military leader as its main character might have certain appeal, but it is limited to those who have an interest in that field. It's much more interesting to see an everyday man or woman caught in some horrific web that seems nearly impossible to escape. That's you and me, and that's much more interesting.

Ultimately, before you reach the final pages of your novel, the middle must wind down. After all the action and good vs. evil you've written, your protagonist will either succeed or fail in his efforts to conquer his demons. This is where you must make a very crucial decision: will there be a walk-off-into-the-sunset Hollywood ending, or will evil get in the last word? Well, that all depends on your future intent. In my novels *Dead Souls, The Demonologist,* and *Deep in the Darkness,* my main characters faced not-so-happy demises. Why is this a considerable element? Look at truly successful horror movies, such as *Rosemary's Baby, Night of the Living Dead,* and *Hellraiser.* These all ended with the bad guy getting his way. Although there was a means to justify the ends, the open endings allowed for sequels to be made (or written). Although this important piece of the puzzle ultimately falls into the ending of your story, it's in the middle where you must start laying the groundwork, by once again foreshadowing the possibility of evil's triumph over good.

In my novel *The Demonologist*, God must side alongside Satan in order to defeat a growing power capable of defeating them both. It's here the reader has to wonder how all can possibly end smelling like roses when there's such adversity in the light of all that is good. It's a swirl of oil in the water quite capable of igniting at any time, hinting at a twist of an ending that may very well punch the reader in the gut when he's not looking. Horror writers do this often, and they do it well.

Every successful horror story has a beginning, middle, and end. Although all three components are crucial for successful storytelling, most of your hard work will be focused on the middle. It's where your set-up leads to, and where you'll build important elements that ultimately command your conclusion. Of course the perfect middle to any horror story depends on how well you write it, and there are many different styles in which to approach your story. But remember this: for a middle to be successful, it doesn't truly matter whether you write your story in first person or third person point-of-view (although this is certainly a defining element to your story). What does matter is that you keep in mind throughout your novel's development that the middle is your main course, and that a main course is something a hearty meal cannot exist without.

And neither can your horror novel.

The middle of your novel is, without doubt, the meat of the matter.

CHAPTER 3

J. F. Gonzalez

The Grand Finale

J. F. GONZALEZ is the author of a dozen novels of horror and dark suspense including *Hero* (with Wrath James White), *Primitive, The Beloved*, and the fan favorite *Clickers* and *Clickers II: The Next Wave* (with Mark Williams and Brian Keene respectively). His short fiction is collected in three volumes, with a fourth (*The Summoning and Other Eldritch Tales*) due shortly from Delirium Books. He also works as a screenwriter, a technical writer, and a web designer. For more information visit his official website at www.jfgonzalez.com.

Not too long ago, I was asked to collaborate on a novella with two writers I admire very much—Gary Braunbeck and John Everson. In the course of the collaboration, due to the nature and thematic structure of the tale, I was given the ending. If you get the chance to read the piece in question (Knock Knock, *Doorways Magazine*, Fall 2008), this will make perfect sense.

It helped that I already had the basic plot, character sketches, and the first two thirds of the story already completed by my co-authors before I started writing my section. But I want to share a very brief excerpt from the story for this lesson:

> "Alex, you were the guy who started (a story) with your ending and worked backwards."

Some writers *do* start with the ending and work backwards. It starts with the concept of something usually dreadful already having happened to your character and asking yourself "How did this character come to be in this situation?" or "Why did such an awful thing happen?" Once you answer those questions you can generally work backward and, in turn, present yourself with a slew of other questions like: "How did Billy's girlfriend lose her teeth?" or "Why was Duke such an angry guy?" or "Why did Bobby conjure that demon in the first place?"

Arriving at endings from a more linear path works the same way. You follow the next logical event or train of action, or you come up with something really out of left field that will knock your reader senseless. You follow these plot threads along to the next scene, and so on, until you wrap up the tale in a neat, nifty conclusion.

Oh . . . but you don't have a neat, nifty conclusion.

You have no idea *how* to end your story or your novel.

I see.

Well, that's why I'm here.

In very simple terms, an ending to a story, whether it is a short story, novella, or a novel, should serve as the *conclusion* to your narrative. There should be one scene, or perhaps a series of scenes, that serve as the final climax that will contain a big payoff. How that payoff is played out can be achieved in three types of endings, found in every genre:

The "They Lived Happily Ever After Ending."

The "Twist Ending."

The "Cliffhanger Ending."

There is a fourth and fifth ending for horror stories, which I'll call the "It Lives! Ending" and the "Gruesome Ending," respectively.

Let's address the first three.

The first one, "They All Lived Happily Ever After" (or TALHEA, my obviously bad acronym to avoid all those keystrokes), is not only the most commercial, it is the most satisfying to the majority of readers. In horror fiction it is especially useful and effective since your characters (and the reader) are put through hundreds of pages of blood-curdling fear, heart-stopping suspense. Characters the reader will come to love get put through perilous situations and, in many cases, they are killed in horrible fashion. If you've got a particularly gruesome novel dealing with some intense subject matter and you end it on a downbeat note instead of something more uplifting and happy, many readers are likely to not pick up another book by you.

It's no surprise that many of the books you find occupying the top positions in the *New York Times* Bestseller's list end happily. Even in the realms of horror fiction, those works that conclude with some kind of TAL-HEA ending can make the coveted *NY Times* List. Dean Koontz comes immediately to mind and, in my opinion, he uses this technique very effectively. You feel for his characters, you like them, and you want them to survive. And very often they do. Changed from whatever horrifying experience they've been through, made stronger by it perhaps, but they've survived and they definitely live Happily Ever After.

The works of Stephen King usually wind up on the *Times* Bestsellers list, too. However, unlike the novels of Dean Koontz, King is more daring. King has no problem killing off well-liked, major characters you think are going to survive. Sometimes events play out in his fiction you never expect to happen. Sometimes he pushes the reader's buttons by dealing with controversial material. Sometimes his books don't end on such a happy note. Despite this, many of his books end up with at least one (sometimes more) main protagonist making it through to the end. They don't always live happily ever after, but he often plants the notion of hope that they will.

The "Twist Ending" is something more commonly found in the works of mystery fiction, especially who-dunnit's, but it can be found in pretty much every genre. The "Twist Ending" is self-explanatory; the conclusion is unexpected, perhaps even shocking, but manages to tie everything together. The elements that make up the "Twist Ending" should be explained by both major and subtle plot points in the story, and through character interaction and dialogue that occurs earlier. Most importantly, the "Twist Ending" should provide a lasting impact on the reader long after the story has been read. Writers like Fredric Brown and Robert Bloch were masters at this. Pick up any short story collection by either writer and you'll see what I mean. Or witness the ending of Bloch's novel *Psycho*. Readers and film audiences in 1959-1960 weren't prepared for the shocking revelation that the psycho on the loose at the Bates motel was actually Norman Bates himself who, in his psychotic state, adopted the mannerisms, speech, and dress of his mother, who was kept very carefully off-screen throughout the duration of the movie (and book) and was rendered so realistically that we accepted her as a genuine, *real* character.

The "Gruesome Ending" can often be combined with the "Twist Ending." *Psycho* comes to mind again. So do the novels of Richard Laymon (especially *The Cellar, The Traveling Vampire Show* and countless others), Edward Lee, Michael Laimo, and, on occasion, Stephen King. Case in point: remember the ending to *Pet Semetery*? Dr. Louis Creed is sitting in his kitchen after having buried his wife in that cursed cemetery and he hears the door to the house open, then the shuffling footsteps followed by the scent of decay . . . and then the hand of his wife falling lovingly on his shoulder along with her dead voice whispering that single word: "Darling."

I still get the chills when I think of that ending.

The "Gruesome Ending" is exactly that—it's designed to enact a visceral reaction. If done well, it should provide a lasting impact on the reader long after they've put the book down.

The "It Lives! Ending" is very popular in most horror novels and is pretty self-explanatory. The "It Lives! Ending" consists of a short chapter (usually an epilogue) showing the protagonists resuming their lives after the gruesome events of the story with a hint that the evil they've battled still lives on. It could be temporarily disabled somehow (by occult means or whatever you come up with), but capable of returning again. The evil could have moved on or could be in hiding, unbeknown to the main characters your readers have come to know and love. Whatever the case, you must convey to the reader that this evil could rise again someday. Good examples of this type of ending can be found in Jack Ketchum's *Off Season*, Richard Laymon's *The Cellar*, and my own novels *Clickers* and *The Beloved*.

The "Cliffhanger Ending" is the type of ending readers either love or hate. The "Cliffhanger Ending" can also be called the "Open-ended Ending." Meaning it ends at the conclusion of the final act at the crescendo of a heart-stopping action scene. A recent example of this is the ending to *The Rising* by Brian Keene. If you have not read it I won't spoil it for you, because to write about the technique Brian used for this particular ending will give the entire story away. Readers used to nice, neat conclusions hated the ending, but readers like myself who enjoy and appreciate daring works responded favorably. *The Rising* ended at a perfect cliffhanger moment where not only questions are raised, but the entire ending is left open to interpretation.

If you want to use a "Cliffhanger Ending" in a novel you must make sure you leave it somewhat open-ended. The very nature of a "Cliffhanger Ending" is to give the reader the impression that the adventure is going to continue on (they also provide a good starting point for a sequel). With that in mind, it's okay to leave some elements of the story open-ended, but not *too* much. Give them enough to make them want to think for themselves, perhaps come to their own conclusions as to how the story ended.

Cliffhangers are most effective for ending chapters in your novel. The best examples of this can be found from novels written for the pulp magazines, especially those published between 1920-1940. It was essential for pulp writers to put their main characters in desperate situations, to have them face impossible odds, and to end each chapter with a sense of *oh my God, what's going to happen next*? It made you turn the page to see what happens in the next chapter, and for those novels that were serialized (a common practice to get the public to buy the next issue), it was imperative the writer end their chapters with a cliffhanger.

Ending chapters on a cliffhanger is not nearly as necessary today as it was in the pulp era, but it's still imperative you end each chapter in a way that compels the reader to keep turning the pages. For that, you need a compelling story and you need to be able to write well enough to keep the reader hooked.

What's that? If cliffhangers aren't as necessary today, what's the best way to end a chapter?

Good question.

Not all novelists work this way so I'll only relate what works for me.

When I sit down to write a novel I already have a good basic sketch of the plot already mapped out. I have brief paragraphs devoted to how each scene plays out. Using this as a guide, I write the novel with the notion that each scene's synopsis will more or less serve as my chapter guide.

This doesn't always work out, however. Sometimes a scene plays out longer than I'd like. Sometimes certain elements important to the book's plot come up and I need to address them in the context of combining them into a single chapter. Sometimes I see the opportunity in the narrative to end a chapter at a heart-stopping breaking point, knowing I can pick it up again in the next chapter, or even a later chapter.

To be honest, there is no right or wrong way to end chapters in a novel. Think of chapters as simply breaking the story up. The beginning of the first chapter could accomplish several things: introducing characters, establish the setting, and then we end the chapter by raising the stakes somewhat. The following chapter addresses those stakes and carries the story further, perhaps introducing a plot element. That chapter should end with another raising of the stakes, and so on.

Chapters are nothing more than section breaks in a very long story—a novel. Each break ends with a raise of the stakes in the plot, further advancing the narrative and keeping the reader turning the pages. An excellent example of this is Robert R. McCammon's *Speaks the Nightbird*. Each chapter of this novel concludes this way—sometimes the stakes are raised in a life-or-death situation, sometimes they merely bring to light certain issues or questions in the plot that compel you to turn the page to the next chapter to find out what happens *next*.

Always end a chapter with the notion that you want to lead the reader on so he or she will want to find out what happens next.

And at some point you will come to that inevitable end where you will have to utilize either the "They Lived Happily Ever After Ending," the "Twist Ending," the "Gruesome Ending," the "It Lives! Ending," or the "Cliffhanger Ending" in the finale of your novel.

Whatever that ending may be, make sure it arises logically from the novel's plot.

Make sure it satisfies you as a writer.

When I finished my novel *Survivor* I realized the ending was bleak. It was a good one, and I liked it, but it depressed the heck out of me. So what did I do?

I wrote an entirely new ending.

A happy ending.

I wanted my characters to overcome the trauma and evil they'd experienced. I wanted them to learn from it, to face up to their actions, but I wanted them to be magically okay afterward. I wanted them to have a good life.

That was the personal side of me speaking. The writer side of me, though, told me that ending was wrong. It wouldn't work out that way in real life, so there was no way my readers were going to buy it.

My editor felt the same way.

So we kept my original downbeat ending.

Why? That original ending was more true to the novel.

You should never *force* an ending. If you've come to love your characters but certain events in your story's plot have taken you to a point where you're afraid things might not pan out very well for them, it's best to let the narrative spill out the way it's supposed to. Trying to write a forced happy ending will not only be very obvious to your reader, it will probably anger them. Some stories require happy endings. When it happens, a happy ending can be a wonderful thing. I personally like happy endings. But sometimes, as in real life, things don't work out the way we'd like them to. And in those cases a happy ending will just be forced and out of place.

So don't do it.

Is it important to know how a story is going to end before you start writing it? Sometimes. Especially if you have an image or an idea for how your story will end. It gives you a goal to shoot for, and as your story progresses it helps shape your potential ending into something more solid, helps make it more concrete.

Many times, though, you will have no idea how to end your story.

And that's okay.

All you have to do is keep writing. Let the story flow. Let it progress; let the characters carry it along. Let their actions determine the plot, the theme, and if you let the story write itself the ending will come to you naturally.

And when you get to the ending it might even surprise you.

And if you get to that point you've done a good job.

CHAPTER 4

Gary A. Braunbeck

Connecting the DOTS

GARY A. BRAUNBECK is the author of 10 novels and 9 short story collections, 1 non-fiction memoir, and has edited 2 anthologies. His work has garnered 5 Bram Stoker Awards, an International Horror Guild Award, 3 Shocklines "Shocker" Awards, and a Black Quill Award from *Dark Scribe Magazine*. To learn more about Gary and his work, please visit www.garybraunbeck.com.

Every so often I will come across a review of one of my novels or stories wherein the reviewer accuses the piece of being "sentimental." While that used to frustrate me no end, I've learned now to be amused when this happens (after all, who wants to waste their time reading a horror story that bothers to create an emotional core?) because I remember the words of Oscar Wilde: "A sentimentalist is one who wishes the luxury of exploiting an emotion without paying the price of actually *experiencing* it." Honest emotion can only be labeled "sentimental" when it's glaringly obvious that the writer is *manipulating* you in order to achieve a single, desired effect, one with no room for variation or for being left open to individual interpretation.

I've been very lucky in the course of my career in that readers and many of my fellow writers feel I have a certain knack for creating emotionally rich, compelling, three-dimensional characters. When not being accused of sentimentality, I'm often asked how I manage to do this, so I thought I'd go over some of the methods I employ for characterization, and then—to illustrate how I try to apply these methods—deconstruct a scene from my story "Union Dues" that numerous readers have told me is one of their favorites.

Please bear in mind that these methods are those that work best for *me* and are not being offered as absolutes or—God forbid—a template that will guarantee you'll get the same results. There *is* no such template; creating a multi-layered, believable, sympathetic character is, like everything else one learns about writing, a matter of trial and error.

It is also a deeply *personal* matter, one that demands the writer be completely honest with him- or herself when creating a detailed map of a character's emotional landscape. If you, as a writer, can find it in yourself to face the honest feelings in your own heart and convey those feelings through those of your characters, you will achieve that rare feat in horror: to create a truthful sense of a character's grief or joy, triumph or remorse, courage or cowardice, loneliness, redemption, any and all of the above, and then lead them and the reader through the very worst of it, transforming them through acceptance, and leaving the reader with a deeper appreciation for their lives and everything that is a part of those lives.

I know that sounds like a tall order, so let's make it even more impossible and bring in this thought from the late novelist John Gardner (*Grendel, The Sunlight Dialogues*): "You must write (each story and novel) as if you are trying to convince someone not to commit suicide."

There is, believe it or not, a point of reconciliation between the somewhat detached compassion in Gardner's directive and the facade of nihilistic darkness in horror fiction, and it hinges almost solely on the ability of the writer to unblinkingly convey honest feeling. (This point of reconciliation can be summed up in—curiously enough—thirteen words, and we'll get to those later.)

But first, let's talk a little bit about acting.

Lauren Bacall tells a marvelous story about her acting debut opposite Humphrey Bogart in 1944's *To Have and Have Not*. Bacall had never acted before, but her head was stuffed full of these overly-glamorous preconceptions about how "stars" behaved (gleaned from devouring an endless diet of film fan magazines of the time), so when the moment came for her to make her entrance in her first scene and utter her first line, Bacall danced through the door into the room where sat Bogart (the perennial cigarette dangling from the corner of his mouth), made a wide, elegant sweep of the room as if modeling a dress on a fashion runway, and then all but swooned at Bogart's feet before delivering her first line as if she were singing an aria.

With the exception of director Howard Hawks, everyone on the set either burst out laughing or—following Bogey's example—groaned and rolled their eyes heavenward. Bacall, mortified, began to flee the set, but was stopped by Hawks. Bacall asked him what she'd done wrong, and instead of listing the at least 3,240 things she'd screwed up, Hawks told her to look at what she was wearing (an old blouse and slacks), pointed to the door she'd waltzed through just a few moments earlier, and said: "Think about where you're coming from—not just about from where *in the house* you're coming from, but also from where in your *life*. And then ask yourself how and why all of it has led you to walk through this specific door at this specific moment and enter this specific room. Because it's all connected, and you need to make sure that we can *see* all of that before you even open your mouth." 65 years later, Bacall still insists that those instructions from Hawks remain the single finest piece of direction a young actress could have hoped to receive at the very start of a career.

Hawks' words remain as wise today as they were in 1944. It's not just the things he told Bacall, but also the things he *didn't* tell her; like why, for instance, her character wore an old blouse and slacks, or had chosen those particular shoes, or how she knew it was safe for her to be alone in a room with a man she'd never met until this moment.

Being a fervent believer in String Theory, I cannot help but smile at Hawks' having told Bacall that "…it's all connected…" because those three words should be framed and hung over the desk of every fiction writer. From the smallest of gestures to the most grandiose of Shakespearian soliloquies, nothing happens within the microcosm of a story that is not somehow connected to everything that came before or that will follow. I came to this realization not through writing, but during my time as a professional actor.

For the better part of a decade—between the ages of 19 and 30—I worked as an actor, mostly summer stock and dinner theatre, with extra work in a movie and television miniseries, and was actually *paid* to pretend I was someone else. During those years, I worked with an assortment of other actors, all of whom had their own approach to interpreting the particular role in which they were cast.

The late Laurence Olivier was a self-proclaimed "technical" actor—he worked from the outside in; he would find a walk, a speech pattern, various mannerisms, etc. through which the character would reveal itself to him. While rehearsing a Noel Coward play in which he played a prissy English lord, Olivier was having difficulty getting a handle on the character. This semi-famous story reached its happy ending when Olivier, passing by an antique store, happened to glance in the window and see a walking stick for sale. He went in to the store, picked up the walking stick, and the moment it was in his hand, he *knew* the character. (The walking stick, by the way, was described by Olivier as "…one of the ugliest, most ostentatious things…" he'd ever seen, but he knew that his character would think it was classy and tasteful.)

I worked with a lot of technical actors. I was one myself. I also worked with a lot of Method actors. Method actors are an ongoing gift to the world from Constantin Sergeyevich Stanislavsky, an actor, writer, and director from Moscow who created an approach that became the vanguard for tackling the psychological and emotional aspects of acting: the Stanislavsky System, or "the Method."

Method acting requires that, if an actor is to portray fear, he must remember something that once terrified him and use that remembered fear to instill reality and credibility into his performance. The same with joy, lust, anger, confusion, etc. Stanislavsky's Method also requires that the actor know *everything* about his- or her character, usually by having the actor write a short "inner history" for their character, details of their lives that—while never used on stage—would nonetheless give the performance even deeper authenticity.

In *theory*, Stanislavsky's Method is an amazing tool for an actor. It requires the complete submersion of the Self into the body, psyche, and thoughts of another person so that an actor's performance rings of the truth.

I use the phrase "in theory" above because, in my opinion, too many actors use Stanislavsky's Method as an excuse for self-indulgence masking itself as research. Don't misunderstand—when you get a Method actor like Marlon Brando (in his prime), Paul Newman, Dustin Hoffman, Sean Penn, Meryl Streep, or Bob Hoskins (to name a small handful) who have the discipline and wherewithal to employ the Method to all its power, you can have something glorious.

But I didn't get to work with any of them. I got to work with Method actors who would spend *weeks* researching and writing their "inner history," demanding that I address them only as their character (even when off stage), and never, *ever* make light of anything at any time. The prime example of how Stanislavsky's Method can be turned into rampant silliness happened when I was doing a stage production of *Sherlock Holmes* and had to do several scenes with the actor playing Dr. Watson. (I played a slimy little safecracker named Sidney Prince.) The actor playing Watson had written a 75-page "inner history" for Watson, researched hand-to-hand combat methods used by British troops during the Boar War, studied medical procedures practiced in London in the 1800s … and when the curtain rose each night, audiences were treated to his imitation of Nigel Bruce for the next two-and-a-half hours.

But that's not the silly part. The silly part always happened off stage, right before the third scene of the second act (where Watson confronts Prince). As he and I waited for our cues, the actor playing Watson would drink a cup of vinegar. I asked him why, and this, word for word, was his reply: "Because, Mr. Prince, dealing with you leaves a bad taste in my mouth."

Time to run, not walk, to the nearest exit.

I finally came to the conclusion that for me, as an actor, Stanislavsky's Method was useless. Every Method actor I had worked with wound up giving stiff, overly-mannered, obvious performances (in that it was obvious they were "acting"). I don't know that I'll ever do theatre again, but if I do, I'll use the same "technical" approach that I always used.

But while Stanislavsky's Method might be useless to me as an actor, it was priceless to me as a writer. I still approach characterization, especially during the early stages of a story or novel, from a technical standpoint, almost always falling back on Stanislavsky's Method when it comes time to add emotional depth and authenticity to whichever character is coming to life on the page—and I won't commit a single word to the page until said character is someone I immediately recognize as an old friend.

I start with two simple questions, questions that are going to strike you as being a bit silly on the surface, but questions that, for me, reveal so much more than what is simply seen: *How much milk does he or she use when having a bowl of cereal?* and: *How does this character put on his- or her coat?*

Let's say that this first character uses just enough milk to barely cover the cereal, thus ensuring that both milk and cereal will be finished at the same time with nothing left in the bowl but the spoon. That's the technical starting point, the outside. Now, let's walk over and look a little closer and ask, *Why do they do this?* They do this because they don't believe in waste; they're not the type to dump the last bit of milk down the sink after the cereal is gone. (And if there *is* any milk remaining, they either lift the bowl and drink it, or set the bowl on the floor so the cat can finish it.) *Why do they not believe in waste?* Because they can't afford to *be* wasteful. They work long hours at a job that manages to pay the bills, the rent, and buy a set amount of groceries each week, but no excesses, no luxuries, no eating out or going to the movies or buying a new CD ... ergo, no wasting of the milk.

This also suggests that this character may not be the happiest person you've ever met; after all, if they have to be this frugal with milk, then that frugality has to extend to every other aspect of their existence, as well, and with that comes an endless string of commonplace worries that, taken individually, may not seem like much, but cumulatively drain a lot of enjoyment from life.

Looking even closer, we see this character is sitting at a kitchen table that also doubles as the dinner table, because he or she lives in a three- or four-room apartment; a nice-enough place that's affordable if not fancy. I'm willing to bet that stashed up in one of the kitchen cupboards is a set of china cups and saucers left to them by a dead relative, cups and saucers that they only use on special occasions, like those rare instances when they have company. I'll also bet you that on this character's chest of drawers in the bedroom we'll find a jar filled two-thirds of the way with an assortment of spare change—mostly pennies, dimes, and some quarters—that this character is planning on using to buy themselves a nice little something-or-other once the jar is full, maybe treating him- or herself to a night out, dinner and a movie, or buying a new pair of dress shoes at Target or K-mart.

I could keep going but I think you've got the idea. And it doesn't matter a bit whether or not *any* of the information from the above paragraphs makes it into the story because I am now well on the road to *knowing* this person; and the better I know them, the more authentic and believable they will be to the reader, and we will have achieved what Stanislavsky's Method demands: complete, unflinching, undistilled truth when depicting the human condition of the character in question.

All of this discovered because of a simple visual nuance.

All of this revealed from looking at a bowl of cereal ... because it's all connected.

Nearly every story I have written has begun with an image of the central character doing something mundane, but it's *the manner* in which this mundane task in *being* performed that instantly tells me a great deal about them.

Just as a creative mental exercise, try this: the next time you go out to a club, movie, party, or restaurant, over the course of the evening choose five people at random and watch how they both remove and put on their coats. Does this person treat their coat with care, removing it slowly, one arm at a time, and then draping it carefully over the back of their chair (making sure that the lower part doesn't touch the floor), or do they just all but let it *drop* off of them, and then thoughtlessly sling it over the back of a chair without a second glance, even though a full one-third of it is now spread out on the floor?

As far as putting the coat back on, watch this, as well. Do they exercise care when they do this (again, one arm at a time, slowly), taking time to smooth it out a bit once it's on their body, or do they make a bit of a show out of it, swirling it around their shoulders like Zorro's cape and then jamming their arms into the sleeves with such wide flourish there's a good chance they could take out someone's eye should that other person be standing too close?

This can tell you a lot about your character, albeit in broad strokes, but that's where characterization starts. The character who takes care of their coat, who is careful to remove it and hang it off the back of the chair so no part of it touches the floor (and who also exercises quiet care when putting it back on) reveals several things through these visual clues: this coat is something that has *meaning* for them—it may have been a gift from a family member who is no longer alive (it may even have belonged to that family member, it's your call); it may have been something for which they had to save money every month in order to purchase because they don't have a lot of disposable income (Hmm—could this person also be our frugal eater of cereal?); it may be that this coat is one of the few things they feel they look good in; or it may be that this is the only coat they own. The possibilities are endless.

But here is the one thing that you'll know immediately: this is, in all probability, a shy person, one who wishes to blend in as much as possible so as not to draw attention to him- or herself. This is a person who will be all too happy to *join in* the conversation, but will rarely begin one of their own volition. Whereas the other person—the one who just tosses the coat down without a second thought and then makes a bit of a show when putting it back on—this person is not only an extrovert, but also quite probably someone who has never really known what it's like to *work* in order to possess the basics (like said coat). The coat may have been a gift from a parent (who is still probably alive, and thus able to provide them with a new coat when this one becomes trashed by having half of it draped across the floor so many times); it may be just one of several coats they own, so what do they care?; or it may be that—like our other person—this is the only coat they own, but because they need to foster this devil-may-care persona among their friends, they treat it with indifference ... until, of course, it's time to leave, and putting it back on allows them to be showy, thus making sure they remain the center of attention.

Like I said, these are broad-stroke examples, but it's a way to begin. Other factors must be called into consideration in order to enrich this scenario; the age and sex of the character in question; the *kind* of coat he or she is wearing: is it something expensive or off the rack at Target or Walpurgis-Mart? Was it tailored specifically for them? And what are the specific circumstances under which he or she is wearing the coat? (I imagine that our first character would exercise the same kind of deliberate care with their coat whether he or she were with a group of people or eating alone—and wouldn't it be interesting if our second character, when alone, treated their coat with the same care and *didn't* make a show of putting it back on? It's fun how this works, isn't it?)

Now peel back another layer from the surface: imagine what's in the pockets of each character's coat. Going with the original conceit that our first character is a shy person who, for the sake or argument, was given the coat as a gift by a deceased parent (perhaps the last gift this person ever received from said parent), they're not likely to stick a used candy bar wrapper in one of the pockets because they couldn't immediately find a trash can after polishing off … what? (Ask yourself that: what kind of a candy bar would this person prefer, or would they like candy at all?) I imagine that our shy person would keep a pair of gloves in the pockets (for when the outside temperature gets cold) and perhaps their car keys, but little else. Simple and uncluttered.

By contrast, our second character would have receipts, loose change, car keys, two or three wadded one-dollar bills they've forgotten are even in there, half a dozen phone numbers scribbled on slips of paper, and a partially-eaten candy bar from six months ago which is growing a fungus that is starting to breathe and develop a rudimentary language.

Okay, so now you've got a character, one who captures the reader's attention (and hopefully sympathy, as well) through a simple visual nuance, whether it be with the cereal or with the coat. Questions are forming in the reader's mind because they want to know more about this character than what the writer has implied or what they as the reader have inferred, and the best way to further peel away the deeper layers of this character's emotional landscape is to have him- or her interact with another character. This where the real fire starts burning, because this is where we begin to draw the correlations and further reveal how everything is linked.

We begin connecting the DOTS—the Definition of the Self that every character carries with them, that hangs about their neck like either pearls or chains, and determines how they will interact with everyone else populating the microcosm of the story.

In my workshops that focus upon dialogue and the DOTS, I offer up several examples of the Definition of the Self as done by myself and other writers, but hands-down the one that I use the most comes from *The Twilight Zone* episode "The Changing of the Guard," written by Rod Serling, the first writer whose words moved me in a profound way.

In this beautifully-written episode the late Donald Pleasance (in a luminous performance) portrays Professor Ellis Fowler, an aged teacher at an all-boys boarding school. As the school begins closing for Christmas vacation, Fowler is informed by the school's Headmaster that after fifty-one years of teaching, he is being forcibly retired. The news devastates Fowler, who's known nothing but the halls of the school and teaching for his entire adult life.

Back home, his housekeeper later discovers him in his study, looking though old yearbooks and reminiscing about students he's taught over the years. In the midst of this nostalgia he suddenly stops, removes his glasses, and delivers to his housekeeper the following Definition of the Self:

> "They all come and go like ghosts. Faces, names, smiles, the funny things they said or the sad things, or the poignant ones. I gave them nothing, I gave them nothing at all. Poetry that left their minds the minute they themselves left. Aged slogans that were out of date when I taught them. Quotations dear to me that were meaningless to them. I was a failure, Miss Landers, an abject, miserable failure. I

> walked from class to class an old relic, teaching by rote to unhearing ears, unwilling heads. I was an abject, dismal failure—I moved nobody. I motivated nobody. I left no imprint on anybody. Now, where do you suppose I ever got the idea that I was accomplishing anything?"

In reality, you'd have to practically strap someone to a chair and threaten to start pulling teeth in order to get them to express themselves so directly and eloquently; that is why your characters give you the priceless gift of rejecting *that* kind of reality and replacing it with your own; in the fictional world, your characters *can* define themselves to themselves and to others this directly, this poetically, this un-self-consciously. And when you know each character's Definition of the Self, you will begin to sense how those individual DOTS will connect to one another when they meet in the story.

I should also note here that a Definition of the Self can be a brutally direct one (as in the quoted *TZ* excerpt above), or it can be an indirect definition, one that is hidden within their words when they speak of someone or something other than themselves.

Connecting the DOTS gives depth to relationships (or the lack thereof); it establishes and escalates conflict; it peels back the layers of your characters' psyches because of what they reveal or struggle *not* to reveal to the others; and—perhaps most importantly—it will establish the emotional core and tone of your story. It doesn't matter if you use everything you know about the character; simply by *knowing* all that you do about them, so much will come across through a simple gesture, a small visual nuance, the way they smile … or treat their coat and eat a bowl of cereal. And once that emotional connection is made, readers will follow your characters through anything and always remain by their side; even if the character in question does something less than noble or kind. The reader will care about your character, they will sympathize—even empathize, and they will *understand* what motivates and drives that character. In short, you will have brought about a communion of sorts between reader and character—perhaps the greatest reward a story can give.

So, a quick review: establish character through visual nuance, then through their Definition of the Self, then through their interaction with other characters and *their* DOTS (be it a direct or an indirect definition) so that relationships and conflicts can arise naturally and give birth to that elusive beast called "plot."

Now let's see how well I practice what I preach. Below is an excerpt from my short story "Union Dues" that originally appeared in *Borderlands 4*. The scene in question comes about ¼ of the way into the story, and it's a scene (as I mentioned earlier) that numerous readers have singled out as one of their favorites. My wife thinks it's the one sequence that best illustrates what all my work is ultimately concerned with. I am just amazed that after *fifteen years* this is one of the few scenes that I've never had a desire to go back and "fix." It still holds up, I think.

As we go through the scene, I'm going to insert some bold-face comments pointing out visual nuances, where the DOTS are established, where they collide to illustrate conflict and establish relationships, and how connecting the DOTS compels the shifting dynamics within those relationships.

In the scene, Sheriff Ted Jackson (a recurrent character in my *Cedar Hill* stories) has come to the house of Darlene Kaylor on the same evening when a massive riot between striking factory workers and scab laborers has left several people dead—including Darlene's husband, Herb, with whom Jackson was a close friend. Jackson was also the person who helplessly watched Herb Kaylor die in a manner that defied logic, reason, or explanation. Jackson has come over to pay his respects and see if there is anything he can do for Darlene and her son, Will—but he also needs to have a few questions answered. Darlene invites him into the kitchen, where she fixes them both a cup of coffee. We come into the scene when Jackson asks the first of his several questions:

"Darlene," he said softly, staring down into his coffee cup, **(Visual nuance: he can't look her straight in the eyes because he still feels at this point in the story that he *should have* been able to do something to save Herb, so the nagging guilt and shock of what he witnessed makes it impossible for him to look Darlene—or anyone else—in the eyes for the first 2/3 of the story, so here, he stares into his coffee.)** "I hate to ask you about this but I gotta know. Why was Herb working the picket today? He wasn't supposed to be there again until Friday."

"I swear to you I don't know. I asked him this morning right before he left. He just kind of laughed—you know how he always does when he don't want to bother you with a problem? Then he kissed me and said he was sorry he'd got Will into this and he was gonna try to fix things."

"What'd he mean?"

"He got Will on at the plant. Was even gonna train him." She shook her head and sipped at her coffee. **(Visual nuance: Darlene shaking her head. There is a sad resignation in her that something like this was bound to happen, and now that it has, it seems nearly absurd to her—especially considering what she's about to tell Jackson—so she shakes her head.)** "You know Herb's father did the same for him? Got him a job workin' the same shift in the same cell. I guess a lot of workers get in that way. Didn't your father work there, too?"

Jackson looked away **(Visual nuance: same reason as before)** and whispered, "Yeah."

"Place is like a f——' family heirloom," Will stood up in the doorway.

Jackson turned to look at him as Darlene said, "What did I tell you about using that kind of language in the house? Your Daddy—"

"—was stupid! Admit it. It was stupid of him to go down there today."

Darlene stared at him with barely-contained fury worsened by weariness and grief. "I won't have you bad-mouthing you father, Will. He ain't"—her voice cracked—"here to defend himself. He worked hard for his family and deserved more respect and thanks than he ever got." **(Indirect Definition of the Self: by characterizing her late husband as a hard worker, she reveals a little of her deep admiration for Herb.)**

"Thanks?" shouted Will. "For what? For reminding me that he put his obligations over his own happiness, or for getting me on at the plant so I could become another pathetic factory stooge like him? Which wonderful gift should I have thanked him for?" **(Another Indirect Definition of the Self: by characterizing his father as a "factory stooge" and then contemptuously asking which gift he should be thankful for, Will reveals his anger at—if not contempt *for*—his father.)**

"You sure couldn't find a decent job on your own. Somebody had to do something."

"Listen," said Jackson, "maybe I should come back—"

"When was I supposed to look for another job? Between running errands for you and helping with the housework and cleaning up after Dad when he got drunk—" **(Wandering off the highway for just a moment, can you see here how dialogue when used in tandem with the DOTS gives you the opportunity to slip in necessary background information that, had it been presented any other way, would have come off as forced or awkward?)**

"I think you'd better go to your room."

"No," said Will, storming into the kitchen and slamming down his coffee cup. "I'm eighteen years old and not once have I ever been allowed to disagree with anything you or Dad wanted. You weren't the one who had to sit down here and listen to him ramble on at three in the morning after he got tanked. To hear him tell it, working the plant was just short of Hell, yet he was more than happy to hand my ass over—" **(The first part of Will's direct DOTS)**

"He was only trying to help you get some money so you could finally get your own place, get on your own two feet. He was a very giving, great man."

"A *great* man? How can you say that? You're wearing clothes that are ten years old and sitting at a table we bought for nine dollars at Goodwill! Maybe Dad had some great notions, but *he* wasn't great. He was a bitter, used-up little bit of a man who could only go to sleep after work if he downed enough booze, and I'll be darned if I'm gonna end up like—" **(The second part of Will's DOTS)**

Darlene shot up from her chair and slapped Will across the face with such force he fell against the counter. **(The exchange between Will and Darlene that preceded this unexpected act of violence on Darlene's part illustrated the shifting dynamics in their relationship—the balance of power, of who was in control of the situation and conversation, kept going back and forth, and Will's direct DOTS collided with Darlene's Indirect definition to create and heighten conflict, all of it leading to this inevitable desperate act on Darlene's part to silence her son's contemptuous words about her dead husband.)** When he regained his balance and turned back to face her, a thin trickle of blood oozed slowly from the corner of his mouth. His eyes widened in fear, shock, and countless levels of confusion and pain.

"You listen to me," said Darlene. "I was married to your father for almost thirty years, and in that time I saw him do things you aren't half man enough to do. I've seen him run into the middle of worse riots than the one today and pull old men out of trouble. I've seen him give his last dime to friends who didn't have enough for groceries and then borrow money from your uncle to pay our own bills. I've seen him be more gentle than you can ever imagine and I've been there when he's felt low because he thought you were embarrassed by him. Maybe he was just a factory worker, but he was a decent man who gave me love and a good home. You never saw it, maybe you didn't want to, but your father was a great man who did great things. Maybe they weren't huge things, things that get written about in the paper, but that shouldn't matter. It's not his fault that you never saw any of his greatness, that you only saw him when he was tired and used-up. And maybe he did drink but, for almost thirty years he never once thought about just giving up. I loved that ... that *factory stooge* more than any man in my life—and I could've had plenty. He was the best of them all." **(The first part of Darlene's Direct DOTS)**

"Mom, please, I—"

"—You never did nothing except make him feel like a failure because he couldn't buy you all the things your friends have. *I* wasn't down here listening to him ramble at three in the morning? *You* weren't there on those nights before we had kids, listening to him whisper how scared he was he wouldn't be able to give us a decent life. You weren't there to hold him and kiss him and feel so much tenderness between your bodies that it was like you were one person. And almost thirty years of that, of loving a man like your father, that gives you something no one can ruin or take away, and I won't listen to you talk against him! He was my husband and your father and he's dead and it hurts so much I want to scream." **(The second half of her Direct DOTS)**

Will's eyes filled with tears. "Oh god, Mom, I miss him. I'm so ... sorry I said those things. I was just so angry." His chest began to hitch with the abrupt force of his sorrow. "I know that I ... I hurt his feelings, that I made him feel like everything he did was for nothing. Can't I be mad that I'll never get the chance to make it up to him? Can't I?" **(The final part of Will's Direct DOTS, and the moment where his Definition of the Self merges with that of Darlene's.)** He leaned into his mother's arms. "He always said that you gotta ... gotta look out for your obligations before you can start thinking about your own happiness. I know that now. And I'll ... I'll try to ... oh, Christ, Mom. I want the chance to make it all up to him ..."

Darlene held him and stroked the back of his head, whispering, "It's all right, go on ... go on ... he knows now, he always did, you have to believe that…." **(And here, where the DOTS connect, the core tone of the story is revealed; one of resigned sadness and regret, where individual sins of omission overpower even the strength of immediate grief.)**

If you've not read "Union Dues," this excerpt should give you some idea that it's perhaps not the happiest story ever written, but I like to think that the emotions at the core of the piece give it the ring of truth, of authenticity, of a story (and storyteller) that grapples with honest feeling instead of trying to manipulate the reader.

And you can employ Stanislavsky's Method here and turn it on yourself: How many of you reading this have been lost in depression, or sadness, or lingering grief, or loneliness, or doubt, or any of the thousands of shadowed corners in the human heart where even the blackest darkness would look like a star going nova, and found some moment of comfort in a book or short story that you've read?

And, yes, you *bet* that this can apply to horror fiction. I'm not talking about that old happy horsecrap that says imaginary horrors help us to better deal with the real but, rather, how the very act of reading something that raises anxiety or provides a good chill reaffirms the *immediacy* and *necessity* of your own existence.

If some part of you is still willing to *choose* to be frightened, or disturbed, or repulsed, then this same part is embracing life by embracing fear: if you can still be scared, then you still think life has value and meaning; and if you still think that life has value and meaning, then there is still hope in your heart.

What greater gift could a storyteller hope to pass on to his- or her readers?

This is why you, as the writer, have to present your characters' emotional cores as truthfully and naturally as possible. And if you are willing to access your own feelings—especially those you have difficulty expressing to others—and gift them to your characters, then your characters will take those honest emotions and, with you as their guide, adapt them to their own situation within the microcosm of the tale in which they have been cast. Because just as everything that happens within that story is connected to what came before and what will follow, *every* aspect of the story is connected to you, the writer, and if you're not willing to express honest emotions to yourself, your characters aren't going to do it for you, and your readers will be faced with a piece of work that—while it may be technically dazzling—has only a cold hollowness where its heart should be.

So connect the DOTS and let the honest emotions be expressed by the imaginary people and things in your story—even if those imaginary things live in dark corners and aren't sometimes particularly pleasant or uplifting.

And here's the thing I promised, the point of reconciliation between John Gardner's earlier directive and the holy chore of writing the best kind of horror fiction: As long as there is fear of the darkness, there will be hope.

* * *

Keeping in mind what we've examined here, allow me to present you with someone:

Female. Mid-30s. Her coat is wool, with a removable lining. It's tan. It's in very good condition and, in fact, might be thought brand-new until you get close enough to see that it's at least ten years out of style. She removes it carefully after entering the restaurant (she's alone) and instead of draping it over the back of her own chair, places it lengthwise across the other chair at the table, so that the collar is just hanging a little over the back of the chair, and the bottom of the coat hangs a little ways past the seat of the chair, nowhere near touching the floor. She's wearing a wedding ring, but it's on the ring finger of her *right* hand. She takes her cloth napkin and spreads it across her lap, then smoothes it out. She picks up the menu, takes a small sip from her water glass, and begins reading. If you watch closely, you can see that her hands are trembling slightly.

What's her story? You sense it, don't you? Maybe you already *know* her story. So …

Time to start connecting the DOTS.

CHAPTER 5

Tim Waggoner

And Horror the Soul of the Plot

TIM WAGGONER'S novels include *Nekropolis, Cross County, Darkness Wakes, Pandora Drive,* and *Like Death*. He's published over one hundred short stories, some of which are collected in *Broken Shadows* and *All Too Surreal*. His articles on writing have appeared in *Writer's Digest, Writers' Journal* and other publications. He teaches creative writing at Sinclair Community College in Dayton, Ohio, and is a faculty mentor in Seton Hill University's Master of Arts in Writing Popular Fiction program. Visit him on the web at www.timwaggoner.com.

There's a great Kids in the Hall sketch about a writer whose first novel is titled *Boo!* When readers open the cover, there's only one page inside with a single word on it: "Boo!" Readers react in shocked surprise, and then grin in delight. We see the author on a successful bookstore tour promoting *Boo!* which has become a national bestseller, scaring millions. Eventually, the time comes for the author to write his follow-up, and he's struggling to come up with something that can possibly equal his previous literary triumph. Finally, inspiration strikes, and he sits down to write *Look Out! There's a Spider on Your Back!* He shows the manuscript to his wife, she reads it, and immediately tries to brush off an imaginary spider crawling on her back. Then she embraces her husband, confirming that he's done it again.

What makes this sketch so funny, of course, is the notion that anyone could actually read a horror story and literally be terrified by words on a page. So maybe we writers of the dark fantastic can't truly scare anyone, but that doesn't mean we shouldn't do everything we can to give readers a great story that uses the emotion of fear as a central narrative element. But the Kids in the Hall sketch reminds us that real surprise—experiencing the new and unexpected—is what we should strive for in horror fiction, and one of the best ways to achieve that is to develop a strong, fresh plot.

Give Count Dracula a New Suit

This advice might seem to fit better in an article on coming up with ideas for horror stories, but it's just as vital when it comes to plotting horror fiction. It's my firm belief that horror—at its best—should make readers uncomfortable. Papa Lovecraft said it best: "The oldest and strongest emotion of mankind is fear, and the oldest and strongest kind of fear is fear of the unknown." Concepts or imagery that once were fresh (or in another word, unknown) can, through imitation and repetition, become well-worn tropes, with poor Papa's mythos being a prime example. In the case of horror fiction, familiarity doesn't breed contempt so much as it does staleness. You can always tell when a trope has become far too familiar for its own good: whenever you start seeing parodies of it (the *Scary Movie* series), whenever it becomes fodder for adventure stories (*Alien* vs *Aliens*), whenever its co-opted by other genres (can you say paranormal romance and urban fantasy, kids?), whenever it becomes safe enough to start showing up in young adult and middle-grade reader fiction (*Twilight* and a billion imitators), and—last but in the 21st century certainly not least—when it becomes a video game ("Hey, dude, when is the new *Silent Hill* coming out?").

Bottom line here: if you've already read it, seen it, or played it, don't write it. But if for some reason, you decide to work with a standard trope, try to put your own unique spin on it. For example, in my novel *Darkness Wakes*, a group of pleasure-seekers keep an amorphous creature called the Overshadow in a secret club hidden in a suburban strip mall. The Overshadow can directly stimulate the pleasure center of a person's brain—but it will do so only after being given a sacrifice: a living being whose lifeforce it can absorb. At its core, *Darkness Wakes* is a vampire story, but the word "vampire" isn't used once in the book.

So you want to write a zombie apocalypse story? Then instead of rehashing the same old plot, what if you reverse things? What if zombies were beginning to become human again? How would surviving humans treat them? How would those who remained zombies react to them? What if the revived humans remembered every atrocity they committed as cannibalistic undead monsters? How could they live with that?

And that's the plotting power of a re-envisioned trope in action. It opens up all sorts of story possibilities that might never have occurred to you otherwise. So take Dracula out shopping for a new wardrobe. You—and your readers—will be glad you did.

I Could Swear We've Been Here Before

Avoiding the overly familiar goes for the events of your story as well. If readers know what's going to happen next, or worse, if they know how it's going to end, you might as well pack it in and head on home. So don't have your main character get sliced and diced at the end of the story or—please—don't have your main character reveal that he or she has really been *dead . . . all . . . along!* (Cue scary music.) Don't have your character's lover suddenly kill him / eat him / drain his blood or soul / cut or bite off his penis. And twist endings? They ain't easy to pull off, friend, and even when they do work, readers—especially savvy horror readers—know to anticipate at least the possibility of a twist ending. In that sense, the twist ending is a *known* quantity to those readers.

As far as I'm concerned, one of the worst twist endings in horror movie history occurs in M. Night Shyamalan's *The Sixth Sense.* When you have two characters in a scene, and one looks at the other and says, "I see dead people," you don't have to be a genius to figure out how the story is going to end.

If you've got an idea for a twist, consider putting it somewhere else in the story. One of the best examples I can think of is the movie *The Crying Game*. I refuse to spoil the plot twist, but it occurs in the middle of the film, not the end, and it spins the story off in an entirely unexpected direction, and the movie is far more effective because of it.

Don't Save the Best for Last

Many beginning authors end their stories with a culminating image of horror. It's like the hoary old urban legend of The Hook. "And there, hanging from the car door handle, was the murderer's *hook hand!"* (And all the seven-year-olds around the campfire shriek.) But one way to make your plots more original, and open up new directions for them, is to begin with a strong image/concept and build from there.

Clive Barker's "The Body Politic" is an excellent example of this. How many horror stories and movies have centered on the severed hand with a life of its own? Too many, and they usually end with the severed hand attacking someone in the name of vengeance. But Barker's story begins with the premise that hands—all hands: yours, mind, everyone else's—have minds of their own, and they wish to be free of "the tyranny of the body." All they need is a messiah to arise and lead them.

My own story "Long Way Home" resulted when I drafted a tale that ended with the image of a rain of blood falling from the sky. I decided to scrap that story, and started another. Only this time, I began with the blood rain beginning to fall and continued from there to detail a demonic invasion and one mother's desperate attempts to protect her child. The second story was far superior to the first, and all because I finally remembered to take my own advice.

Consider a Change in Direction

If you're in the middle of writing a story and find yourself stuck on what happens next, try this: ask yourself what couldn't possibly happen at this precise moment in the story, and then make it happen. Now I don't mean throw in a plot development that's patently ridiculous: "Bob was just about to enter the haunted laundromat when a giant meteor struck the Earth and destroyed the entire planet, rendering Bob's struggle to save the town from the Demonic Dryer moot." What I'm talking about is to try to shake up what you already think is going to happen in your story. So if in your mind, the next event to occur in your story is that Bob is going to successfully enter the haunted laundromat, what if the door refuses to open and he can't break through the glass? Or what if he does get in but the Demonic Dryer isn't there? What if, when Bob does finally find the Demonic Dryer, he discovers he can't destroy it without releasing the evil spirit possessing it to wreak even greater havoc?

There's an added bonus to this technique. Not only will you get your story moving again, it'll head off in a direction you never suspected—and that means your readers won't have expected it either.

How is Just as Important as What

Beginning writers often believe that event is all there is to plot. This happens, then this happens, then this happens, The End. But the *way* a story is told is just as important as the events that comprise it.

Edgar Allan Poe's "The Tell-Tale Heart" is a classic example. The story is narrated by a murderer who is explaining the meticulous steps he took to commit his crime in order to prove that he isn't insane, because—he insists—only a man with a rational mind could have carried out such a plan. Watching the unnamed narrator's pretense of sanity slowly slip away as he tells his tale *is* the story.

A more modern example—to revisit zombies once again—is *Zombie*

Haiku by Ryan Mecum. It's the story of a man's transformation into a cannibalistic zombie as written by himself in small snatches of haiku-like bits, which is all his decaying mind can manage to record. Though the book is shelved in the humor section of bookstores, there's nothing funny about the tale. The fragmented method in which the narrator relates his descent into savage mindlessness is absolutely chilling.

So the next time you're plotting out a horror tale, don't forget to think about the how. After all, there's a reason it's called story*telling*.

All Fiction (Including Horror) is Mystery

Here's one of the most important things you'll ever learn about writing fiction: readers don't literally want you to tell them what happens next; they want to discover it for themselves. To see this principle in action, check out the following:

Joanne saw the wardrobe mirror sitting in the middle of the floor. Looking back at her from inside the glass was the image of her dead husband.

He knows what I did, she thought, and he's come back to get even with me!

That's the bad kind of telling. Everything is spelled out for the reader clearly and plainly—and it is dull. Now what if I put the mirror in the attic and add a stronger atmosphere of mystery?

Joanne set foot on the bottom rung of the ladder and reached up to grip one of the higher rungs. She looked up at the square of darkness that was the attic entrance, and she could've sworn she felt a cold draft emanating from the shadows. Just my imagination, she lied to herself, and she almost believed it.

Slowly she began to climb, taking one rung after another, until her head passed through the attic entrance and into the cold darkness beyond. She felt like a diver cautiously entering frigid black waters in which anything might be waiting for her . . . anything at all.

I could keep going, but you get the idea. In the first example, I simply told you what happened. In the second example, I let you experience mystery through Joanne's point of view, and you make discoveries at the same moment she does. The second version may not garner me any Stoker nominations, but it's a sight more effective than its predecessor. When this technique is done well, the author isn't merely telling the story. The author has given readers the tools necessary to tell the story to themselves, in the same way that a composer provides music for a musician to play. A writer is the composer, the reader is the musician, the story is the sheet music, and the instrument the reader plays is their imagination.

So when plotting your story, make sure to keep the mystery going and allow your readers plenty of opportunities to discover the story for themselves.

And in Conclusion, Class . . .

Hey, if writing horror—*good* horror—was easy, everyone could do it. But if you want to create tales that not only entertain readers, but challenge and unsettle them, then give them the delightfully creepy *frisson* that only horror at its best can provide, then make sure you tend to your plot and tend it well.

CHAPTER 6

Scott Nicholson

What's The Point and Who's On First: Character POV

SCOTT NICHOLSON is the author of seven novels, including *The Skull Ring* and *They Hunger*. His new story collection is *Scattered Ashes*. He's also a screenwriter and his novel *The Home* is in development for a feature film. A paranormal enthusiast, Nicholson works as a journalist in the Blue Ridge Mountains of North Carolina. His Web site is www.hauntedcomputer.com.

One of the quickest ways to jump to the top of the slush pile, engage the reader, and create emotional connections with your fictional characters is to pick the right point of view and stick with it.

Until you shift.

But make sure you're comfortable with your POV, because it provides the eyes that see the story, the brain that processes information, and the perceptions, discoveries, and change that underscore the theme.

At the simplest level, "point of view" is exactly what the words say: the point or perspective from which you are writing your tale and the character view from which the story's events are witnessed. At the most complex level, point of view involves varying shades of penetration, from the aloof God's Eye of the omniscient to the analytical introspection and immediacy of first-person POV to the adjustable focus of an ever-shifting third-person lens.

The omniscient viewpoint was popular in much pre-Twentieth Century fiction, almost to the point where the reader expected the writer to intrude at any time and remind everyone that this, after all, was just a story. It was not uncommon for the narrator to write "We" passages, where the writer and reader shared information that the characters didn't have. In Sheridan Lefanu's seminal vampire tale *Carmilla,* the author jerks the reader forward through months of events simply by pulling aside the curtain for a few paragraphs and draining a lot of the story's suspense.

While omniscient storytelling does allow for convenient continent-hopping and time-hopping, it also saps tension. God by its very nature must be fairly dispassionate, since good and evil get equal billing and mercy must be measured out in small doses. So God's view is broad and remote and allows the reader to know everything almost before it happens, like a camera on the theater ceiling. The advantage of omniscience is you can move the set pieces around while showing the entire stage, but modern fiction counts heavily on the reader's identification with the characters.

Second-person POV is so rare and artificial that it immediately draws attention to itself. The story is told as if the reader is the narrator, though most times the author wants the reader to identify with the main character through a mirror or distancing mechanism. Stewart O'Nan's masterpiece *A Prayer for the Dying* uses the technique to great effect. The protagonist, a sheriff and undertaker in a small town ravaged by disease, pursues horrible tasks in an almost matter-of-fact way, leading up to a wrenching finale that makes you relieved you didn't get deeper inside the protagonist's heart.

First-person POV works well in situations where you want the reader to inhabit the main character's skin. This works well in building suspense, which is why it is fairly common in detective fiction where the reader uncovers clues along with the protagonist. But it also is highly effective in horror, especially when the character slowly realizes something unnatural or perverse is taking place. The shared sense of dread and anticipation keeps the reader turning pages.

Edgar Allan Poe used the first person masterfully in his works of claustrophobic horror, often throwing doubt on the narrator's sanity. In "The Tell-Tale Heart," he writes, "If you still think me mad, you will no longer when I describe the wise precautions I took for the concealment of the body." It is one of several references to madness in the brief tale that immerses the reader in the narrator's feverish mind as he alternately seeks to reassure us and unsettle us.

Thomas Tryon uses the technique in *Harvest Home* to show a man moving his family from the big city to the too-quiet village of Cornwall Coombe. As a fish out of water, the "I" character (Ned Constantine) first comes to appreciate the leisurely life of a village that seems lost in time, but then little by little learns the bloody secrets of tradition and ritual. Because this world is new to him, the reader feels the freshness of discovery, but as the relaxing lifestyle becomes ominous by turns, the reader is swept into the drama in a way that might not have been successful in a third-person POV where the reader was privy to the plotting of the village elders along the way.

H.P. Lovecraft often used first-person POV to explore his multiverse of sinister, timeless forces, and his "I" character was often a university professor or educated man who was summoned to check out a scientific curiosity or invited to a strange setting by an obscure relative. However, Lovecraft augmented his "I" characters with other first-person viewpoints, either through characters relating their experiences to the narrator or through journal entries and correspondence read by the narrator.

Lovecraft often dialed out his POV microscope so that his first person was emotionally remote, creating an omniscient feel, such as in "The Shadow Out of Space." In his opening, before the narrator introduces himself, Lovecraft muses on the fragile nature of consciousness: "There are terrors that walk the corridor of sleep each night, that haunt the world of dream, terrors which may indeed be tenuously bound to the more mundane aspects of daily life." In Lovecraft's imagination, the horrors are so large that even an omniscient God might not know them all.

The "I" character can also be used effectively when the narrator is an author, such as in Bentley Little's *Dispatch*. A talented writer must depend on words to not only make sense of a bizarre world but to save his very soul. Sprinkled in the narrative are letters that allow the writer's art to imitate life, or at least the life of the story, in an unselfconscious way.

First-person POV also allows for an unreliable narrator, such as in Jim Thompson's *The Killer Inside Me.* Deputy Lou Ford, if you believe him, is a well-meaning guy who just happens to come upon people who aren't fit to live, and is as amazed as anyone when he is suspected of murder. "Why did they all have to come to me to get killed?" Lou asks with a sense of wonder and a little bit of weariness.

You could argue that first-person POV is the most natural storytelling voice because it's the one you use around the campfire, in the coffee shop, or on the witness stand. You tell the events as they happened, in sequential order, ending with the lesson learned or the unintended consequences that have followed up to the point you are telling the story.

But you could make an equally compelling counter argument that, in fiction, first person is the most artificial form, because, after all, the character is rarely sitting down and typing the story as it unfolds. First person also trims some suspense, since we know the character lives to tell the tale or set it down on paper, though there are notable exceptions such as Deputy Lou Ford and Susie Salmon in *My Lovely Bones*.

Modern commercial fiction overwhelmingly relies on third-person POV, but it's not so simple as "He said, she said, they did this." There are many possible levels of penetration and also varying numbers of viewpoints. Some authors rely on a third-person POV but stick with a single character throughout the book, essentially broadening the effect of first-person by retaining the freedom to move a little outside the character's senses on occasion. This can be deep penetration, where the reader is expected to buy into the character's experience and interpretation of events, to shallow penetration where the character POV is used as little more than a perspective through which the omniscient God is observing the story events.

The writer's challenge is to ensure a character knows only what he or she has experienced and is unaware of something happening simultaneously across town or across the world, unless that character has ESP. The advantage, especially in using multiple viewpoints, is a richer opportunity to express different philosophies and explore different genders, classes, races, and attitudes in the same work.

In Jack Ketchum's *Red,* the protagonist Avery Ludlow is so steeped in the story that Ketchum rarely refers to him by name, often using a hypnotic flow of "he" to keep the reader walking alongside Avery on his path of vengeance. Only rarely does Ketchum refer to Ludlow's thoughts, actually writing "he thought" instead of using italics. Because Ketchum sticks with Ludlow's perspective throughout the book, the reader comes to think like, relate to, and cheer for Ludlow, though Ketchum also creates a masterful distance that raises tension and adds a distinct literary quality to his tale.

In Alexandra Sokoloff's *The Harrowing,* protagonist Robin is the perfect viewpoint character for a haunting, because she's damaged, vulnerable, and already moving into darkness by contemplating suicide. Set in a college dormitory and featuring five main characters, *The Harrowing* strikes a compelling and delicate balance because we come to know the other four characters solely through Robin's perceptions and attitudes, and Robin is in effect "wearing sunglasses at night" and hardly able to see any character in an unbiased light. Since one of the best tools of supernatural fiction is its use as metaphor for a troubled mind, it's no wonder that people who see ghosts seem to be crazy.

The tightening of a specific viewpoint can be particularly effective in letting one character take over the story. In Ira Levin's classic *Rosemary's Baby,* the married couple of Rosemary and Guy Woodhouse start with equal weight, full of the excitement of a new apartment. The reader is kept at some distance as the couple interacts with their friendly but eccentric neighbors. But as Guy becomes a little estranged from Rosemary and she becomes more resolved to have a child, Rosemary slowly takes over the viewpoint and all the events orbit her. Much of the story's horror is conveyed by Rosemary's arc from skeptical, frightened, and isolated wife to an accepting and loving mother. By the end, the viewpoint has become so thoroughly Rosemary's that Levin dispenses with "she thought" altogether as she looks upon her infant: "He couldn't be all bad, he just couldn't; even if he was half Satan, wasn't he half her as well, half decent, ordinary, sensible human being?"

Epic fiction works best with a shifting third-person POV, in which the writer and reader jump from head to head as the story unfolds. Stephen King is the master of this technique, as he is with most techniques. Probably the most stunning display is in *The Stand,* where dozens of major characters take their personal journeys, whether into darkness or light, and line up against one another in the biggest showdown of all. From the mute Nick to the damaged Nadine, King effortlessly jumps from voice to voice and scene to scene, weaving together the myriad individual threads into a complex magic carpet. Not only do his characters have distinctive speaking voices, they also think and perceive the world in a certain manner, often applying wildly different meaning and interpretations to the same set of events. King's gift and talent is in keeping each character absolutely consistent, jumping into each skull with the confident ease of a soul-hopping spirit while never letting the reader feel lost or overwhelmed.

King is also talented enough to break free of third-person and go into omniscient viewpoint, such as in *Salem's Lot,* where he interrupts the timeline of the story 100 pages in, just as the corpses start to mount, to talk about New England seasons. Addressing the reader directly, putting you squarely in the story, he writes, "If the only sound is the slow beat of your own heart, you can hear another sound, and that is the sound of life winding down to its cyclic close, waiting for the first winter snow to perform last rites."

The writer's challenge is to know how much information to dole out, balancing the character's story role against the emotional investment the reader must make. One of the hallmarks of badly written horror fiction, and a major contributor to the wide perception of horror as a juvenile, coarse genre, is the mindless racking up of a body count of two-dimensional, cardboard people. That doesn't mean every character must get a viewpoint in shifting third-person; a minor character can be painted in a broad stroke, even a borderline stereotype, while important characters will express more thoughts and participate in more scenes. If you want the reader to care about whether your character lives or dies, let the reader know and understand the character. When your neighbor dies, it's a tragedy; when 1,000 people die, it's a statistic.

It's not just the protagonist's viewpoint that is important, though because of the conservative nature of the horror genre we usually expect Good to prevail and order to be restored. The devil occasionally must get his due, as in "Yours Truly, Jack the Ripper" by Robert Bloch. The short story's "I" character is a psychiatrist who is presented with a bizarre theory that posits Jack the Ripper continued his string of crimes across the decades and the globe. While the ending is not totally unexpected, the cleverness of Bloch's first-person viewpoint actually moves us to suspend disbelief and be swept up in the twist.

Of course, rules are made to be broken, but you better have a good reason for shifting POVs within a book. In William Goldman's *Magic*, the story opens with a first-person line "Trust me for a while." Several pages pass before we learn we are reading a journal entry from *The Wisdom According to Fats* and that the information is presented as a police exhibit in an investigation. While we know immediately that Fats is not to be trusted, because only a liar feels the need to build trust, Goldman takes his time spinning a tangled web that inextricably binds ventriloquist Corky Withers to his dummy Fats in one of the classics of psychological horror. The other significant third-person viewpoint comes from Corky's romantic interest, who serves as sole witness to the odd relationship's deterioration. In the end, neither Corky nor Fats knows which is which, a skillful manipulation of point of view.

The most basic goal of POV is to make life easy on the reader. While some authors can deftly shift POV within a paragraph, if you fill a page with shifts, the reader is likely to give up rather than reach for a scorecard. If your POV is clear and identifiable from the start, and the character's voice is distinct, you have hooked your reader enough to buy time to get to plot and eventually theme. Upon that foundation, you can stack the bricks as you wish, remembering that if you use shifting third-person POV, the characters' voices are not "your" voice and each must have individual quirks, traits, and flaws. At its most fulfilling, writing allows you to become the viewpoint character and experience the vicarious thrill of getting to know a stranger from the inside out.

Then step aside and let your new friends breathe and walk and play until they reach the end, then invent and meet new ones.

CHAPTER 7

Thomas F. Monteleone

"We don't get too many strangers around here . . . ." Or: Using Dialogue to Tell Your Story

THOMAS F. MONTELEONE is a four-time winner of the Bram Stoker Award. He has written television scripts for *American Playhouse*, George Romero's *Tales from the Darkside*, and a series on Fox TV entitled *Night Visions*. He is also the author of the bestseller, *The Complete Idiot's Guide to Writing a Novel.*

Your mission—should you choose to accept it—is to learn how to create great dialogue when you're writing your tale of horror, dark fantasy, or suspense. Along with characterization and plot, dialogue is the third indispensible pillar underpinning all good stories.

Making your dialogue believable, natural, and transparent are crucial to writing effective, saleable fiction of any kind. And although I'm going to be targeting writers of dark genres with this particular piece, what I want to talk about is applicable to all kinds of narrative, regardless of category.

More than a few years ago, when I used to read the slush pile for a couple of SF magazines, I learned a lot about what comprised good writing *and* bad writing—and how to spot each kind quickly. And believe it or not, one of the very first indicator flags was *dialogue*. Use your own experience as a reader, and you'll see what I'm talking about. If you start reading a story or novel and the dialogue seems less-than-natural, you notice it almost *instantly*. A writer can't hide bad dialogue. When he doesn't have his characters speaking in a convincing fashion, it sticks out like the hood ornament on a LaSalle.

Good dialogue is what I call transparent—it is so natural, so effortless the reader doesn't take much notice of it, other than to *accept* it as the correct way these folks in the story should be talking. Good dialogue is absolutely essential in fiction for many reasons—primarily because it is the most expedient route to creating living, breathing, believable characters. A writer who handles the conversations of his characters with skill and confidence will be *very* readable. Your audience will identify with people they can understand, and that's what writing dialogue is all about—connecting characters with readers.

Invite Them In

That means making your story accessible and engaging to your reader. Employing dialogue at the beginning of your story invites the reader to *participate* in the story by eavesdropping on two people already having conversation. Dialogue, especially on a story's opening page, looks inviting on the page. Open, airy, lots of white space, which connotes plenty of room for pause and thought.

Nothing more daunting than to flip through a book and see page after endless page of dense, thickly worded paragraphs. I've noticed the novels of many contemporary South American writers have this general appearance. Not much dialogue at all. Such novels don't *look* like a fun read. They suggest a slow, plodding effort that means real *work.*

As soon as it's introduced, dialogue makes a short story or a novel more accessible. Conversation and speech are universal to most of us and we don't need to be schooled on it, or prepared for it. Readers understand it and accept it immediately, unconsciously. Hey, if it sounds right, they never question it.

Keep Up the Pace

When you can integrate your dialogue into your narrative passages, you'll notice right away how much *faster* things seem to be going. There's a kind of kinetic energy of give-and-take in the conversation between characters, which acts like an engine, always moving forward.

You should use this innate characteristic especially in your opening scenes or chapters because you want to pull your readers into the story and keep *them* there.

Talking in the Real World

Another characteristic of good, effective dialogue is its proximity to the way people really talk. But it's a fine line to walk, because if you attempt recreate *in toto* the words of real people in their everyday exchanges, you will be dealing with lots of quoted passages that could be largely incomprehensible.

Real speech is often fragmented. The next time you're out in the neighborhood at a restaurant, a store, a subway, or anywhere else where people are interacting, I want you to get into a little old-fashioned eavesdropping. Try to be subtle, make believe you're doing something else, like reading or working a crossword puzzle, but all the while zone-in on the conversations of those around you.

It won't take you very long to notice something we usually take for granted. Most of us tend to talk in a kind of verbal shorthand. It's very informal, and marked by pauses for breath, laughter, a lack of the correct word or phrase, the ever-present "uh," etc. People also tend to speak in the present, even if they're describing something that already happened (" . . .so my boss says: 'okay, who's leaving the lights on in the copy room again?' and I says: 'King Kong, you dummy!'").

You'll also notice a peppering of mild profanities, slang, contractions of words ending in "ing," and a distinct lack of the mention of anybody's *names*. This last one is interesting, because you'll often see characters named in written dialogue—writers think it's a slick trick for letting us know who's talking to whom. (It's *not*.)

Hard Working Words

Dialogue serves many functions in your narrative and most of them are things you probably never think about. That's because dialogue is such a natural and expected part of storytelling. But you need to make yourself aware of the many tasks your dialogue can make easier on you. Let's take a look at the most obvious ones:

1. - *Exposition.*

This is just a fancy way of saying the words of your characters can be a quick, efficient way to impart information—about what's happened "offstage" or before the action of the story commenced (sometimes called the "backstory"), or any historical elements, etc.

2. - *Sets the Mood.*

Each scene has its own mood and tone, its "feel," and you can use dialogue to help create this by having your character's talking about something that will evoke a particular mood. Mention of an old spooky legend will set up feelings of fear or suspicion in the reader, just as the description of a handsome stranger could suggest starry-eyed romance and anticipation. Or what about an exchange of dialogue where the characters are insulting or threatening one another? That creates an immediate mood and tone that implies danger, trouble, or at the least, tension.

3. - *Reveals Character.*

Ever hear those radio commercials warning us "People judge you by the way you speak" (and then urge us to buy their Vocabulary Builder or whatever . . .)? They're actually right. Speech patterns, vocabulary, and grammar can tell us tons of info about a person—in a very short amount of time and space.

If your character is a construction worker, his dialogue should be differentiated from that of a physician. Sometimes a character's occupation can be revealed and reinforced through their dialogue. A career military man may have his speech colored by armed service phrases and buzz-words. A college professor may have a tendency to use words a little too lofty or stiff for everyday use.

The major point here is to be aware of who your characters are and *listen* to the words they employ. Ask yourself: "Would they really talk like this?"

If the answer is "Maybe not . . . ." then you need to work on their (your) dialogue.

4. - *Individualizer.*

This is closely related to character, and is a simple, effective way to make your character stand out from the crowd. Through dialogue, you can give him (or her . . . yeah, yeah . . .) a habitual speech mannerism, or a favorite phrase, that becomes a familiar and comfortable identifier. Maybe the hero's sidekick always has a habit of saying "believe-you-me" when he wants to emphasize something. Or maybe the antagonist likes to describe troublesome things as "unsavory." You can also indicate attributes and "character type" by using terms that help root a character in a particular region of the country. A soft drink in Boston is called a "tonic," but it's a "soda" in the Carolinas. See how it works?

These are simple examples of countless ways to spice up your characters, make them less ordinary, more believable. Keep this function in mind, and your characters will thank you for it.

5. - *Tension.*

Dialogue tends to be most compelling when it conveys a sense of *something wrong*. Think about it. If, during your eavesdropping missions, you overhear two people talking about something they both like, or a topic in which they're in total agreement, their conversation is usually nowhere near as intriguing as the dialogue of two people who *disagree.*

That's because disagreement suggests tension, or worse, *conflict.* And if you know anything at all about narrative, you know conflict is the essence of storytelling. So, if you can arrange for your dialogue to convey some of that dramatic tension or outright conflict, you're deepening the texture of your narrative *and* pulling the reader in.

You can also use dialogue to *increase* tension and create suspense by foreshortening information one character may be *telling* another. Either by interruption or design, whatever your dialogue provides (or withholds) can torque up the tension in your story.

Different Ways to Say It

Although there aren't any hard and fast delineations of dialogue into formalized "types," I think it's worth looking at the variety of ways you can have your characters talking. And again, the method you choose should match the character's other traits.

1. - *Standard English.*

This is what you'll have the average character speaking. The language and style we hear everyday on radio, TV, and in the world of commerce and education. In that sense, it's a speaking style that becomes kind of "invisible" to us. We accept it as conveyor of information, but it doesn't draw attention to itself.

This is the kind of dialogue we normally see employed in novels. If you learn how to write it well, no one will ever notice . . . and that's a *good* thing.

2. - *Dialects*

A dialect is a variant of any language usually associated with geographic or socio-economic factors. The first time I drove around the country, I remember stopping at a little gas station in Georgia and the attendant asked me if "th'all" was okay. I had no idea what he was talking about, and after a few minutes I dumbly realized he'd said "the oil," which a mid-Atlantic person pronounces "oy-uhl."

This is dialect, friends. It's hard to capture in print unless you have a finely attuned ear for it, and a knack for depicting it with phonetics that aren't egregiously in the way. If this sounds like I'm saying to use dialect sparingly, I guess I am. Writing good dialect is *not* for everybody. Some writers can pull it off and some can't. My advice is to let your editor tell you if you're any good at it, and whether or not you even need it to enhance a particular character.

And just in passing, I should note there's also a distinct difference between the way English is spoken in the United States and the United Kingdom. I can remember the first time I was in London, I saw a sign in a restaurant which said:

English Spoken Here. American Understood.

That kind of says it all, don't you think?

3. - Monologue

Another distinct type of dialogue is really just one character talking—hence the prefix "mono." It occurs when one of your characters needs to make a speech, a proclamation, or that most literary of monologues, the soliloquy.

This is specialized dialogue that you have to be wary of. If too many of your characters are launching off into long, singular passages of exposition, you run the risk of boring your reader. Even if you simply *have* to have a scientist explain the plasma physics that is causing the molten core of the earth to suddenly become solid, it's probably a good idea to break up his delivery with the words of another character who either disagrees or doesn't comprehend. Long monologues tend to be speeches, and they just aren't that compelling in print.

If you need a soliloquy, in which a character undergoes some self-analysis or introspection, it's probably a good idea to present it as a series of internal *thoughts*. Having a character talking aloud to himself usually comes off as plain silly—because people don't really do it very much at all.

4. - *"Street" Talk*

This one is interesting because it's so tempting and accessible. Modern novels tend to use language less formal and less structured than in previous generations, but without an overwhelming tendency to rely on colloquialism or slang.

I think it's a good idea to be aware of contemporary speech patterns and mannerisms, and to even employ them with control and judgment. If you listen to the way people speak, you'll probably notice that about half of them drop the *ing* and replace it with *in';* and more than 90% use contractions resulting in *can't* and *didn't* rather than *cannot* and *did not.* In fact, many people only use the non-contracted versions when they want to express specific emphasis.

This is an example of our language evolving. It's subtle and non-planned or calculated. It's simply happening. Your job is to notice these changes and fold them into your writing, into your dialogue.

You have to exercise a little caution, however, because in this hi-tech, instant-info world, things have a way changing *very fast.* What might have been red-hot and super "in" when you wrote the final sentence could be old news when it gets published less than a year later. Which means your use of trendy, pop-cultural phrases and terminology can heavily anchor your story to a narrow strip of time, thereby "dating" your material. This tends to be off-putting to some readers, who can't see past any universal and timeless truths you may be exploring—because they don't see your story as "relevant."

Stylin'

Okay, let's take a breath and see what we've learned. Now that you have a pretty good idea of what dialogue *is* and some of the jobs you need it to do, I think it's time to take a closer look at the things that will make your dialogue soar above the ordinary.

1. - *Vocabulary.*

There's no substitute for having a wide-ranging vocabulary. And I'm not talking about a huge arsenal of fifty-dollar words guaranteed to dazzle but possibly confuse your readers. Rather, I mean having at your command an ample number of words that, while simple enough, will give your characters enough *different* ways to speak. You want to use a variety of words to keep things fresh, to keep them interesting and to give your characters' dialogue individuality.

I can remember reading a mystery novel once where all the characters kept referring to this part of the house as "the veranda," where a major scene had unfolded and where people tended to gather. Everybody used this word *so much* it started to look like self-parody, and every time I encountered the word, I'm yelling "C'mon . . . *again* with veranda?" This is a case where the writer needed to throw in a few patios, porches, decks, balconies, and even a few lanais. See what I mean?

The last thing I want to say is: it doesn't matter where you get your vocabulary, just that you *have it* at you disposal. I graduated from a Jesuit high school, and they made me take *four years* of Latin, which pretty much ensured a panoply of words for every occasion, but if you've got a nice big thesaurus (the ones in dictionary format are the best) or plug-in software for your word-processing program, or a friend you call when you're stuck . . . no problem. Whatever works for you is great. Just make sure it's working.

2. - *Rhythm and Cadence.*

This is one of the more subtle distinctions between good dialogue and stuff that's just outright clumsy. There's almost no way to describe it; this is the stuff you really need the "ear" for. Sometimes, you have to listen to the *way* people talk rather than what they're saying.

Some people end most of their sentences with a question, or an implied question. Or they ask a question by making it sound like a declaration. Some people use very short, clipped sentences. They respond tersely and in ways that can be mistaken for rudeness. Others run on in flowery and effusive exclamations. That's cadence. Some people speak in a recognizable pattern or syllables, almost like the metered lines of a poem. Everything they say has da-da-dah-di-DAH sequence to it. That's a speech rhythm.

You don't need to consciously attempt to recreate these patterns and mannerisms—just be *aware* of them. The words and the sequences you use when writing dialogue can contribute to unconscious perceptions of realistic versus phony. Your reader may not *know* why your dialogue's not ringing true other than thinking it just doesn't "sound right." Rhythm and cadence might be the issues.

3. - *Variation and Balance.*

More subtlety at work. When you write your dialogue, pay attention to the length and intensity of what your characters are saying. Even if they have a fairly equal amount of information to impart, try to make their dialogue sufficiently *different* to keep it distinctive and always pushing the plot forward.

Having one character ask questions and another answer them sets up a nice balance that can carry things for a while. One word replies contrast nicely with those moments when you needed lots of exposition. If you have both (or worse, *more*) characters all unloading long passages of spoken data-dumping, then you may have a situation where people are no longer *talking* to one another, they're what I call "speechifying." Do I need to tell you that's a bad thing?

4. - *Brevity and Silence.*

These concepts are really refinements and enhancement to the previous one. Don't be afraid to have some of your characters actually say *less* than they should.

Let me explain. You've heard the expression that sometimes *less is more,* right? Well, it really works well in dialogue, because when a character is less than forthcoming with information, emotions, expectations, etc., it creates *tension* in the other respondent characters *and* in your reader—all things you *want*.

When a character doesn't say *anything,* you can sometimes crank up suspense or frustration to an even higher notch. Even though you've probably never considered it, silence is a legitimate aspect of good dialogue.

In the novels of Lee Child, his continuing character—a truly intriguing guy named Jacker Reacher—causes lots of problems after the writer employs this line: *Reacher said nothing.*

Tricks & Techniques

Okay, maybe they're not really "tricks," but I like to think of them as clever verbal equivalents of sleight-of-hand. Read on and you'll see what I mean.

1. - Open With Dialogue

I hinted at this one way back at the beginning of this piece. Early in my career, I remember being at a convention, listening to a panel on writing, and one of the writers offered this tip. If you start off your story or your novel with dialogue, you generate immediate interest because people have to be talking about *something* . . . and your reader is going to want to know what it is. And like I said previously, if you open up with dialogue that suggests an argument or a conflict, that's even more effective.

Even better, open your story with one character asking somebody else a question—a question you may, or may *not,* answer. It's a natural hook that leaves the reader not only waiting for an answer, but also wanting to know who's doing the talking and who's doing the listening.

2. - *Use Humor*

Dialogue is a natural way to inject humor into your story. And by this, I don't mean having your characters telling jokes to each other (although I've seen it tried . . .). Humor can be wry and clever and suggest more than it reveals. The Spenser novels of Robert Parker are extremely good at making the dialogue advance the plot in entertaining fashion.

Humor can be sardonic or it can be broad. Although I would avoid going for the slapstick-ish affectation of characters calling each other by silly names. Irony and satire are also subtle forms of humor that can be created with really good dialogue. You can't go wrong with less rather than more. Subtle is almost always better than over-the-top.

3. - *Signal Phrase*

It's always fun and a bit of a challenge to come up with a catch-phrase or sentence, which can resonate through your novel, and take on more and more meaning as the story inexorably unfolds. This is harder to do than I'm making it sound, but when it happens (largely through good old serendipity), you should be ready for it and recognize for the effective tool it can be.

Stephen King uses this one with great skill. And you can make it your own by jacking up the usage-stakes.

What I'm talking about here is double-meanings, ironic observations, words that eventually turn out to be code for something else, or a phrase whose meaning has been misapplied and suddenly made clear. This sort of thing works well when you had a character saying it all along, and *nobody* has caught on, even though they've been hearing it throughout the novel.

Like I said, most of the time, you'll hit on a verbal gimmick like this by accident, so just be on the lookout for its largely unconscious and unplanned appearance.

4. - *Mannerisms*

You can do this to give your dialogue a little variety. Pay attention to the things people do when they talk—putting an index finger to the chin, talking out of one side of the mouth, licking their lips excessively, or tsk-tsking, etc. By describing the *way* people speak, it helps distinguish one speaker from the other and adds character.

5. - Read it Aloud . . . to Yourself

One of the best ways to know whether your dialogue is working is to read it out loud. I know, this sounds obvious, but you'd be amazed to know how many writers never try it, have never even *thought* of it. I discovered the value of it very early on in my career—when I was at a convention where they'd scheduled author readings.

I listened to some of the other writers reading their own work, and was frankly astounded by three things: (a) most of them could not read for jack, (b) most of them had about as much personality as a newel post, and (c) a lot of their dialogue sounded unnatural and wooden when spoken aloud.

I decided way back then, I would make myself a dynamic reader and performer, and I would always read my dialogue aloud before letting it out of the house. I had discovered the simple truth that dialogue sounds startlingly different coming out of your mouth than it does rattling around inside your melon.

6. - Read Plays

You need an ear for dialogue, of course. But if you also want to develop an *eye* as well, read a lot of stage plays. Or at least enough to get you accustomed to the rigor of telling a story primarily through dialogue, which a play must do at its most basic level. Professional playwrights tend to have dialogue that is economical, yet freighted with tension and power. Spend a little time analyzing what the best of them are doing, then go forth and do likewise.

Don't Go in There! Can't You Hear the Violins?

Okay, even though I'm making this seem like writing dialogue is pretty easy, I have a few final warnings. There are a few simple mistakes and errors in judgment that can befall you, and make your dialogue, well, let's say "less than smooth." Or downright crappy.

1. - *"As You know . . ."*

I see this one in a lot of beginning writers' work. For some reason, they think it's a good idea to have characters updating information or back-filling action that took place prior to the opening of the novel.

The problem with this is obvious: characters are telling other characters stuff *they already know*. And the only reason they're telling the redundant information is because the writer needs his *reader* to know it too. The only thing the characters leave out of their dialogue is the old prefatory "Well, as you know . . . ."

But that doesn't make it any less awkward. Best advice: keep that kind of exposition out of your character's mouths. Figure out other ways to get your back-story told, even if you resort to omniscient narrative or one of your characters reflecting on past events or reliving them in a dream. Just about anything is better than "as-you-know . . ."

2. - *Long Speeches*.

This is an over-use of dialogue that has fallen out of favor. And for good reason—it's boring. Nobody wants to be lectured to, not even college students, and they expect it. Long speeches feel too much like you're getting reprimanded for not knowing something, and a novel is supposed to be entertainment, remember?

I think the only novel I've read which employed the long speech with *any* success was *Atlas Shrugged* by Ayn Rand; and that was only because of the brilliant content of her speaker's words. But even then, the technique blew itself out like a tired storm because the unending torrent of words became too much of a good thing. At that point, I'm pretty certain the author didn't care if her readers knew they were getting a lecture.

I think you and I still need to care. So, if you feel a speech coming on, keep it short and under control.

3. - *He Said/She Said.*

The use of "said" in dialogue is one of those necessary evils. New writers worry about over-using it and if that includes you, my advice to you is to just forget about it. "He said / She said" is simply *there* when you write dialogue; try to think of it as punctuation. And you have to believe most readers just glide right through the words as effortlessly as they do periods and question marks.

Of course, you don't need "said" following every line of dialogue. Watch the exchange of lines, get a feel for it. This is where you need to use your judgment by throwing it in every time you think your readers might need another indicator as to who's doing the talking.

Nobody is really noticing he said / she said. Trust me, okay? And going along with this is a kind of "copyeditor's war" on what is the proper usage of *where* "said" appears in the line of dialogue. Is it: *said John?* Or: *John said*. My advice on this one is whatever feels right is probably okay; and this depends on the rhythm of the sentence.

Another way to identify a speaker is to add a sentence describing a character's action immediately following the stuff in quotation marks.

4. - *No Substitutes.*

Some writers take their apprehension of over-using "said" to a higher degree of paranoia. They decide it's a better idea to use just about *any* word in place of the offender. So the reader is treated to an unending parade of sentences in which speakers never *say* anything. Instead, they *stammer, opine, declare, hedge,* even *laugh* out their words.

Okay, can I tell you frankly? This is just plain awful. Half the time, the said-substitute is a word or word-sound that would preclude the speaker from actually producing speech. (Just exactly how would you "chortle" out a sentence?) I think you get the idea on this one, and the point of it all is easy to remember: said—no substitutes.

5. - *Adverbially Speaking.*

The last and final gaff is yet another attempt by writers to *do something* with that darned "said." They agree to still use it, but they insist on dressing it up with an adverb, which as Mark Twain once said, should be shot whenever we run into one.

So you have endless variations of "he said, slyly," or "she said, harshly," or . . . yeah, you've got it. Again, the advice here is clean and simple and to the point. Just avoid doing this as much as possible. I *know* every once in while it seems unavoidable to get that one little extra piece of description into the dialogue, but keep it to a minimum.

So, Don't Forget:

Good dialogue approximates the way people really speak. To become adept at writing it, you need to pay attention to those around you. You can develop an "ear" for it if you make the effort.

Dialogue is a powerful tool, which can enhance the other elements of your story or novel. Characters can come to life and be distinctive through the dialogue you give them. Everyone should not sound the same. Dialogue can also advance your plot and create tension, conflict, and suspense.

Understand the different kinds of dialogue and learn to use them to create variety and originality. But be careful not to overdo dialect or colloquial speech. Good dialogue is all about balance and rhythm.

And here's the best part—the more you listen to other people speak, the more you read your stories out loud to an empty room, the more dialogue you *write* . . . well, it starts to get like that second or third glass of single malt scotch.

So smooth, you don't even notice it.

CHAPTER 8

G. Cameron Fuller

A Claustrophobic Locked in an Isolated Room: The Power of Setting and Description in Horror Fiction

G. CAMERON FULLER'S fiction and nonfiction has been published in newspapers and newsmagazines, literary and genre periodicals, fiction collections and classroom textbooks. As a book evaluator and editor, Fuller's work has also helped clients win awards and Fellowships, most recently winning a national award—a bronze IPPY, the Independent Publisher Book Award—for the history, *Monongah* (Davitt McAteer, West Virginia University Press). Fuller was on the editorial board of *Writer's Digest* for a number of years and currently writes, edits, and teaches in Charleston, West Virginia.

Think for a minute about the opening scene in *Jaws*. Benchley's novel or Spielberg's movie, it doesn't matter which you consider. Although the novel starts underwater, from the point of view of the shark, and the movie begins on the beach, both versions really get going with the same circumstance: Two swimmers alone in the ocean. One, the woman, is unaware of the other, the shark.

> The great fish moved silently through the night water, propelled by short sweeps of its crescent tail. The mouth was open just enough to permit a rush of water over the gills. There was

> little other motion: an occasional correction of the apparently aimless course by the slight raising or lowering of a pectoral fin. . . . [T]he fish sensed a change in the sea's rhythm. It did not see the woman, nor yet did it smell her.

In the movie, you see the scene from the shark's point of view as it spots the woman swimming above. She is lazily dog-paddling in the night water, and the shark starts to rise toward the woman . . . faster. Then you see the woman, her head and shoulders above the water as she bobs slightly, like a float on a fishing line, and bobs again, stronger, and she suddenly knows what's swimming beneath her, what she has been trapped by in the ocean-night, her look of confusion transforming into an expression of horror.

It's all there in that opening scene. And even though the scene takes place in the wide-open ocean, the setting is constricted, the woman made isolated and powerless by the hugeness of the space around her and the monster shark caught trolling for a victim, a predator in its element. The shark, relentless and implacable, embodies a perfect vicious otherness, but Benchley/Spielberg use settings in *Jaws* to maximize the horror. Close examination of the settings in good horror—and the way settings and characters are described—can reveal many of the secrets behind creating powerful horror fiction.

Consider this fact: Horror is the only genre named after the emotion it evokes. You can doubt whether that was the intention from the beginning, at the dawn of horror fiction. After all, such stories have been known by many different names: ghost stories, tales of the *weird*, of the *macabre*, of the *supernatural* or *psychological*, or—perhaps the best, a term used by H.P. Lovecraft—*fear-literature*.

People have been telling such stories for thousands of years and writing them down for a century or two. In "Supernatural Horror in Literature," a long essay Lovecraft apparently wrote to ennoble an underappreciated genre, the creator of the Cthulu mythos wrote, "Atmosphere is the all-important thing, for the final criterion of authenticity is not the dovetailing of a plot but the *creation of a given sensation* [italics added]." Over the years and through all the stories written, that sensation was considered so important that the entire genre came to be identified with it: horror.

What Lovecraft called *atmosphere* is today more often known as *mood* or *tone*, and it is central to creating the sensation of horror within the reader. The writer of horror fiction faces the task of molding every element of the story—character, plot, setting, exposition, dialogue, detail, and so on—to conjure within the reader the greatest sensation of horror possible. Of all those elements, the most important is *setting*.

Setting can do more to create an atmosphere of horror than anything else about a story. Oh, certainly, plot and character can go a long way, but without the right setting, true horror is rarely achieved. In fact, horror stories—short or novel-length, literary or cinematic—are more distinguished by their settings than are stories in any other genre, with the possible exceptions of science fiction and fantasy.

Edgar Allan Poe and many writers after him have believed that the ideal setting for horror is unitary—singular, isolated, or constricted in some fashion. A great deal of horror develops in unitary settings: the cabin deep in the woods with its radio broken, the tiny island far out to sea, the crippled spaceship floating helplessly in space, the wall gradually bricked in around the helpless protagonist. (Of course, these examples, chosen for clarity's sake, are obvious clichés, but good writers find ways to rejuvenate tired clichés, a few of which will be discussed momentarily.) In this conception, the ideal setting for horror is a small, dark room, the smaller, the better.

A good horror setting must evoke a sense of isolation, with powerlessness and claustrophobia often serving as isolation's companions. Frequently, horror stories begin in an isolated setting (or a setting whose isolation grows as, for instance, radio communications are lost or the only ferry to the mainland sinks). The urgency of the isolation is then heightened as hope diminishes, bit by bit. The horror mounts as each option is foreclosed, as each choice is taken away, in much the same way that Montresor builds Fortunato's tomb, brick by brick, in "The Cask of Amontillado."

Essential to any powerful horror setting is its ability to make the central character(s) feel *trapped*. In that horror-disguised-as-science-fiction movie, *Alien*, Sigourney Weaver and the crew of the *Nostromo* were prisoners in deep space without a means of communication. In *Jaws*, the characters and extras on Amity Island—whether they knew about the shark or not, the reader / viewer did—were prisoners of their own motivations: economic interest or desire for summer fun. Even when a novel or movie has a series of settings, the climax always takes place in a clear, well-defined setting—a gymnasium in *Carrie*; an abandoned house in *Night of the Living Dead*; and so on—often a setting in which the main characters feel trapped.

The impressions made by a powerful horror setting can be so strong that the reader / viewer may believe that the setting dominated the book or movie. The setting's horrifying effect gives the reader the impression that most of the story occurred in that single setting. Often, this is not true, as exemplified by the Stephen King novel *Cujo*. Most people, when asked where *Cujo* took place, will mention the Pinto in which Donna and Tad were trapped. It just *feels* like they were imprisoned in that car for the entire book. Actually, they were in the car for less than half of the book, but King made masterful use of that setting.

The effect of a powerful setting is analogous to the effect of a powerful character. In *Silence of the Lambs*, Hannibal Lecter's presence dominated the book and movie. He has more page-time in the book than screen-time in the movie—due to author Thomas Harris's revelations about Lector's backstory, which were not in the movie—but in both cases, Lector's presence *feels* larger than it is. A strong setting is as integral to horror fiction as are memorable characters like Hannibal Lecter.

Thoughts about the singular setting necessary for strong horror fiction bring to mind a writing theory of Edgar Allan Poe's, one often referred to as the need to *work toward a single effect*. Poe, one of the earliest writers to thoroughly explore horror fiction, believed that every aspect of writing should be focused on a singular goal: "[T]here should be no word written, of which the tendency, direct or indirect, is not to the one preestablished design." He was writing about more than simply horror, but his theory applies to horror fiction.

Many people believe that, despite Poe's essays and letters about his "single-effect theory," he didn't actually write with literary theories in mind. They believe Poe's theories were created after the fact in an effort to legitimize his work. Whether that's true or not, writers should keep the "single, desired effect" dictum in mind when crafting *descriptions* in horror fiction. By choosing the most evocative words, writers can heighten the reader's sense of being *trapped* in a given setting.

John Gardner, prolific author and experienced teacher, stressed the importance of finding the *right* words for description. What he had to say in *The Art of Fiction* is perhaps especially appropriate for writers of horror fiction, whose interest in the strange and otherworldly can sometimes result in descriptions vague or incomplete:

> A scene will not be vivid if the writer gives too few details to stir and guide the reader's imagination; neither will it be vivid if the language . . . is abstract instead of concrete. If the writer says *creatures* instead of *snakes*, if in an attempt to impress us with fancy talk he uses Latinate terms like *hostile maneuvers* in-

> stead of sharp Anglo-Saxon words like *thrash, coil, spit, hiss,* and *writhe,* if instead of the desert's sand and rocks he speaks of the snakes' *inhospitable abode,* the reader will hardly know what picture to conjure up on his mental screen. These two faults, insufficient detail and abstraction where what is needed is concrete detail, are common. . . .

Where possible, writers describe scenes, settings, characters, and events in horror fiction with words that do double duty. They not only accurately paint a word-picture, but also create a foundation for the horror of the story. Some writers tackle the problem head-on, evoking horror immediately; others do so more obliquely, choosing words carefully to allude to horrors to come. Some writers, like William Peter Blatty in his book, *The Exorcist,* do both.

Blatty's first paragraph in chapter one speaks directly of what is to come, although it does so in a tempered way, mirroring the book itself, in which the reader is never sure whether Megan is possessed or suffering from a mental illness—until it's too late. The first paragraph reads as follows:

> Like the brief doomed flare of exploding suns that registers dimly on blind men's eyes, the beginning of the horror passed almost unnoticed in the shriek of what followed. In fact, was forgotten and perhaps not connected to the horror at all. It was difficult to judge.

The second paragraph is more indirect, sprinkling evocative words into a relatively mundane descriptive passage in which he introduces the primary setting of *The Exorcist*:

> The house was a rental. **Brooding. Tight.** A brick colonial **ripped** by ivy in the Georgetown section of Washington, D.C. Across the street was a **fringe** of campus belonging to Georgetown University; to the rear, a **sheer embankment plummeting steep** to busy M Street and, beyond, the **muddy** Potomac. Early on the morning of 1st April, the house was **quiet**. . . . At approximately 12:25 A.M., Chris glanced from her script with a **frown of puzzlement**. She heard **rapping sounds**. They were **odd. Muffled. Profound.** Rhythmically clustered. **Alien code** tapped out by a **dead man**.

Note the bolded words. Words chosen to begin putting the reader on edge appear even before Chris is bothered by the tapping: *brooding, tight, ripped, fringe, sheer embankment plummeting deep*. A glance back at the first paragraph reveals the words *blind, horror,* and *shriek*. Now take a moment to look again at the description above of the shark circling in the ocean. Note the words of menace Benchley chose to use.

One last word about description before returning to setting: Some writers will disagree with this, but when it comes to primary characters, *the less they are described, the better.* Most of the time, especially in genre fiction—horror, science fiction, romance, crime fiction, and so on—the main character becomes functionally a stand-in for the reader. As the story progresses, if the writer is doing the job right, the reader increasingly identifies with the main character.

As a consequence, the reader begins to subconsciously imagine the main character as looking, more or less, like the reader. The writer should avoid making it difficult for the reader to identify by describing the main character in too much detail. The more colorful the main character—weighs 790 pounds, walks with a pronounced limp, speaks in riddles—the less likely the reader will identify. And the less the reader identifies, the less likely the reader will feel what the main character feels as the author calls up feelings of powerlessness, claustrophobia, and desperation. Only a reader who *feels* trapped will know the full horror of the fiction.

Think about settings in the best horror fiction you are familiar with. The same images come to most people's minds: solitary cabins in the woods, deep tunnels and caves, graveyards at night, haunted mansions, defunct and abandoned prisons, crippled spaceships, and so on. Those settings appear easily because most of them have become cliché due to overuse. The author's duty—and a danger here—is to make such settings fresh, if they're to be usable at all.

(In horror fiction, writers often caution against falling into the trap of the *anthropomorphic fallacy*, also sometimes called the *pathetic fallacy*. For instance, rain and darkness are used to heighten tension or evoke gloom. This is not actually a writing error *unless* the writer implies that the raining sky means the heavens are sad. In other words, the anthropomorphic or pathetic fallacy lies in *attributing human emotions to inanimate objects*.)

Writers make such overused settings work nowadays in a couple of ways. Sometimes by examining the specifications of the cliché, the writer can change one or more of them to something unexpected. This can lift the story beyond the cliché. In other words, writers can change the setting somehow until it is *not* the cliché setting readers expect. For example, the creature chasing the main character through the underground tunnels is not trying to kill her but attempting to *warn* her, to save her from some doom that lies ahead.

Another approach horror writers use capitalizes on their ability to transform settings with which readers might be comfortable into frightening and merciless places. The settings start out familiar and comforting, only to darken and become strange: the classy, old-fashioned hotel becomes a maze and a prison; the carnival at night after most of the customers have gone becomes a habitat for freaks and monsters; the patient at the safe and sanitary hospital is taken to its basement world of scalpels and frightening machines. The writer uses the familiar to engineer the strange.

Stephen King has spoken of just such a transformation. He once (at least) told an interviewer he always wanted to set a story in an airport, specifically, in an airport bathroom. Most of us, he said, especially the men in the audience, have had the experience of waiting outside the bathroom as a spouse went in—and had taken forever to come out. King wanted to write the story in which people enter the airport bathroom but never come out. (He just could never come up with a good plot to go with the setting.)

Writers can also make the familiar strange by remembering a fact key to the definition of setting. Even though readers and viewers typically think of setting as a *place*, writers know that all settings actually comprise two components: place *and* time. A house in upstate New York in 2010 is a very different place than a house in upstate New York in 1683. Keeping this in mind allows writers to draw the new and unexpected from the familiar and comfortable. A character might, for instance, step from a 2010 kitchen and into a 17th century living room, or a 23rd century living room, with all the disorientation, isolation, and horror that could well result.

Finally, keep in mind that setting can be so vivid it can be a character in its own right. Sometimes, this is literally true: the hotel room in the Stephen King short story and John Cusack movie, *1408*, is such a character; in *2001: A Space Odyssey*, the space ship slowly becomes the demented and sadistic HAL, who harasses and imprisons the main character, Dave. ("Open the pod bay door, Hal.") Even if the setting is not a full-fledged character, its "personality" can have a strong influence on the plot and characters, as it does in *The Exorcist*, *Rosemary's Baby*, *The Ring*, and so many other horror fictions.

Most of the points of this discussion could be expanded on considerably. Each topic—evoking sensation and atmosphere, setting the story, describing events and characters, transcending cliché, making the familiar bizarre, setting as character—contains details and nuances too particular to address here. Think about them on your own, though. Use your questions and thoughts as springboards to propel you into your own considerations about setting and description in horror fiction.

CHAPTER 9

Rick Hautala

The Hardest Three: Tone, Style, and Voice

RICK HAUTALA has more than twenty-five published books, including the million-copy, international bestseller *Nightstone*, as well as *Twilight Time, Little Brothers, Cold Whisper, Impulse, Four Octobers, The Mountain King* and *The Wildman* (from Full Moon Press). He also has had four books published under the pseudonym A. J. Matthews, including *The White Room, Looking Glass, Follow,* and *Unbroken*. Over fifty of his short stories have appeared in national and international anthologies and magazines. You can read more about him at his hopelessly in need of an update website www.rickhautala.com and in Wikipedia.

Okay, this is where it gets a little tricky …

A lot of storytelling is—well, none of it is really "easy," but parts of it are relatively objective. You have plot, character, setting (time and place). You know, your basic "who, what, where, when" of your story. And before you start writing, you may have figured out your "theme" (the "why" of your story). Sometimes the theme comes first; other times, it comes later. We may have to write the story to know what we mean to say. It's all part of the job.

Like I said, though, all of these are relatively objective.

(Please note again: I didn't say "easy." Coming up with a story isn't always easy; for some of us, it's *never* easy.)

But here we're considering the "how" of your story, and under that umbrella come "tone," "style," and "voice." These three words are often tossed about quite casually, but this is where a discussion of writing gets difficult because these things are so subjective.

Plenty of other writers and critics may disagree with me … Heck, they *WILL* disagree with me. My only defense is that I'm being subjective about something that's … umm … subjective.

So for now, I'll lump all three of these together even though, as we go along, we'll try to make distinctions. The biggest problem I see with any discussion of tone, style, and voice is that we're talking about personal choices (for the writer) and personal tastes (for the readers).

You see, after you come up with an idea for a story—what's it about, who's in it, who's the good guy, who's the bad guy, what's the basic conflict, where and when does it happen?—you have to figure out how you're going to tell your story. This is often the time when writers talk about staring at the "blank sheet of paper" or the "blank computer screen." Maybe the "blank" is in the mind … in which case maybe you shouldn't be writing.

There are some basics, of course. You have to make word choices—syntax, sentence structure (simple, complex, fragments, etc.), punctuation usage (or lack thereof), similes, metaphors, images, details, dialog, diction … all that "fancy stuff" that will make your story come alive.

But this brings me to the first problem I see regarding style.

Now keep in mind, this is coming from a writer who has never been praised or even complimented on his "writing style." I think I know why. I honestly believe your writing style should be like special effects in a movie. Years ago, someone said that the best special effects are the ones you don't even notice. They're seamless … invisible to the viewer. They don't draw attention to themselves because, if they did, they would pull the viewer out of the movie … away from the story.

If a writer's style draws attention to itself, the writer has committed the worst possible sin a writer can commit: He (or she) is getting in the way of the readers' involvement with the story. She (or he) is shifting focus onto "how" he (or she) wrote the story.

I hope you see my problem here?

If there are three elements in the basic equation of storytelling—writer, story, and readers—it's essential that the writer gets out of the way and not insert herself (or himself) between the readers and the story.

Now there are some writers (and readers) who say this is not a bad thing. They even prefer it. And I'd be the first to admit their point of view may be valid. But for me—a reader *and* a writer for whom story is paramount—anything … absolutely *anything* that draws the readers' attention away from your story and puts the attention on you, the writer, is … well … egotistical.

It makes me think of a kid riding his bicycle and shouting: "Look Ma! No hands!" More often than not, that kid will take his attention away from his bicycle riding, lose focus, as it were, and go careening off the road into the pucker brush. His bike ride—which should have been the most important thing, not showing off—will end with tears and bruised knees, maybe even a bruised ego.

Okay. I've mangled that metaphor long enough, and (if you're paying attention) that's "style" because of the words and phrases and images I chose to make my point.

And my point is, you should not be paying attention to *how* I'm getting my point across; you should be paying attention to my point.

Now let's try to get down to some distinctions.

What are the differences between tone, style, and voice?

Good question.

I wish I had some neat, clean answers.

For the longest time—even after I had ump-teen published novels and short stories, I always felt insecure whenever the subject of "style" came up. (I still feel nauseated when the subject of "voice" comes up, but I'll get to that in a bit.)

"What is style?" I'd wonder and ask myself but not dare say aloud because—if I don't know what style is, how can I be a writer? ... I mean a "real" writer?

It all fed into my feelings of insecurity about my own writing and being an imposter—a *poseur*, if you will. My published books and stories would all be discovered to be flukes. (Sorry for the use of the passive voice there. I *do* know better!) If I don't know what style is, I don't *really* know what I'm doing. I should be able to articulate what style is or else get a job at the car wash.

So here goes.

It's easy enough to use a simile and say "style is like your fingerprints." Everyone would tell the exact same story idea in vastly different ways because all that story stuff (plot, character, setting, etc.) are filtered through each individual's unique perspective.

So style has something to do with our individuality, I guess.

Sounds reasonable.

Digging a little deeper (I do have a word limit here), I might even say that style is a combination of all the ways—the verbal or literary quirks—we use to express our ideas and stories.

Side note: My advice to you is: Don't ever let "theme" dominate your story. If it does, you might want to consider a career in politics or the ministry, instead. Preaching rarely if ever works in fiction.

Pretty much the whole deal in writing fiction is to tell a story your readers will get involved in with characters they will come to care about. Hey, they're plunking down their hard-earned money and spending precious time they could be using watching *The Daily Show* rather than reading what you wrote.

Don't preach to them ... (like I am to you right now).

Back to topic.

So let's dance around this topic a bit more. Let's leave style (and voice—I'll get to that last because that's when the claws come out) to consider tone.

Now tone ... I can wrap my head around that a little better simply by understanding that tone is two-part. It's the author's attitude toward his (or her) readers, and it's the author's attitude toward her (or his) subject material ... the story itself.

Easy enough, right?

What is the author trying to do to me, the readers? What emotional and intellectual reactions (the classic "heart and head quandary) does he (or she) want from me? Is she (or he) trying to scare me ... or make me laugh ... or make me think about one or more of life's imponderables ... or get me upset ... or rouse me to action ... or make me feel sympathy or hostility toward someone ... or ... whatever?

Years ago at a convention, I was on an authors' panel where I suggested that there were three basic questions a reader needs to consider in evaluating a story.

1. What is the author's intent in writing?

2. Does the author succeed in his (or her) intent? And

3. What is the relative value or merit of the author's intent?

All good questions, I think. Remember to ask yourself all three about everything you write.

On that panel a female science fiction writer (who shall remain nameless) turned on me like a striking praying mantis about to take the head off its mate and, in front of a rather large gathering, asked me in a vicious tone of voice how I could *dare* presume to know what the author's intent was. I couldn't *possibly* know!

I was flabbergasted.

First, I hadn't been expecting to be taken so severely to task ... especially on a panel of supposedly professional writers by an author I hadn't met or read. (I read some of her stuff afterwards: It sucks.)

I stammered something about how if you didn't know what the author's intent was in writing, then perhaps the author hadn't communicated very clearly, now, had he (or she).

The point of writing—of *good* writing, anyway—is to make yourself clearly understood.

Agreed?

Good. Let's move along.

That seemed like a reasonable response at the time, and the more I think about it, the truer it strikes me.

The author's job is to communicate clearly, not obfuscate things, and the attitude the author takes towards the characters, plot, and theme should be clear. Otherwise, who do I know who to root for in the story?

So tone, I guess, is the easiest of the three.

Now when it comes to how the author feels about her (or his) audience ... well, that's another story altogether, and I think that's where style and voice also enter in.

The simple question is: How do you as a writer view your audience? Do you want to lecture to them (usually a bad thing to do in a story)? Do you want to entertain them ... enlighten them ... tick them off? Do you think they're a bunch of chuckle-nuts who need to be told everything, or do you trust them to figure it out and keep pace as you move along?

That's the second half of tone. And please—never assume a position of superiority and write down to your audience.

In a nutshell, then, style, tone, and voice are choices you make to tell your story. What you put in, and what you choose to leave out.

Sounds reasonable, right?

But this is where it gets tricky because, like the Three Bears' porridge, style can be "too hot," "too cold," or "just right," depending on personal taste and tolerance of heat and cold.

Some writers—especially beginners—want to tell it all. They gush. They slay with verbiage. They overkill. They are what I like to call "word drunk." They relish words and phrases that sparkle and roll off the tongue (or brain) ... at least for them, and they use them liberally. Perhaps too liberally. Continuing my Three Bears metaphor, you can over-season your porridge, and hot, cold, or lukewarm, it doesn't matter; *no one's* going to like what you serve.

This is where we hear that wonderful phrase: the "telling detail."

Now that's one thing a writer has to know about and has to know how to do. That's really the big trick in writing. How do you pick the exact details to tell your story and move it along without drawing attention to every detail and how you're writing them? Remember: You want to avoid taking the readers out of the story.

Don't you?

Rhetorical question: Of course it is.

That's your real job, and trust me—it's not easy. If you're doing it correctly, it's *never* easy.

So my simple advice is: Don't get "word drunk" (or simile drunk or metaphor drunk or image drunk). Resist it at every turn. This is also where we get the "kill your darlings" maxim. Take it seriously.

Hone your story down to the essential, telling details that the readers absolutely need to "get it," and don't spend (some would say "waste") the readers' time shouting: "Look, Ma! No hands!"

The other side to this is the use of spare language and sparse detail. Some readers and writers prefer this. Think Hemingway here, and you'll know what I mean, but there are other greats (like Kurt Vonnegut and Joe R. Lansdale and Ed Gorman to name just three) who write sparse, clean prose that never ... *never* draws attention to itself and never takes the readers out of the story.

Remember: Your goal … your primary directive at all times is to get readers involved with your story. Get out of the way. Don't stand between them and your story.

Can you see how I'm blending and confusing my three subjects here?

For that I apologize, but honestly—I try to *do* this stuff more than I like to *think* or *talk* about it. Like I said, talking about this topic isn't easy.

Now we come to the third subject … voice. And I have to explain why discussion about "voice" makes me throw up into my mouth.

(Okay … I'll admit that image was a tad on the strong side, but if I'm doing what I'm talking about here, that may have created a powerful reaction in you and made a strong, vivid connection between you and my topic … which *is* my goal.)

"Voice," at least as I understand it, is the same thing as style except many writers (especially beginners) treat it as if it is "precious." I mean *r-e-a-l-l-y* freakin' "Precious" with a capital "P."

A lot of writers—all writers think they're unique, right? We wouldn't be writers if we weren't convinced we had some unique gifts, some great ideas and plots and characters and themes that are so interesting we want to—we *have* to share them with the world. We even think they're such good ideas people should *pay* us just for the privilege of reading them.

They do … if we're successful.

So when people talk about "voice," they're talking about how unique and sensitive and perceptive *they* are. They (or their stunningly unique talents) are more important than any stupid old story.

That's simply not what writers should be concerned about. (Sorry for ending that sentence with a preposition. I didn't see a smooth way around it.)

If, as a writer, you want to draw attention to yourself and how frickin' brilliant you are—fine. Go ahead. You'll find readers, I'm sure. But when you talk about "voice," don't ever think you are anything special.

You're not.

Maybe no one else could tell the story exactly the way you do, but if you're more concerned about how *you* sound than you are in getting your story across, I'm sure there are other writers who could tell the same tale much better.

Let's see if we can summarize.

Tone: The writer's attitude toward 1) his (or her) subject material and 2) her (or his) audience.

Style: The words and phrases and images—the language you choose; the sentence structure you use; the details that will (or, if handled ineptly, will not) deliver your story, all the stuff you put into and leave out of your story.

Voice: That's just: "Hey everyone! Look at what a great writer I am!" … in which case, I hope you end up in the ditch with tears, bruised knees, *and* a bruised ego.

I hope this helps.

If you disagree with anything I've said—that's probably a good thing.

Above all, keep writing.

CHAPTER 10

Michael A. Arnzen

Stripping Away the Mask: Scene and Structure in Horror Fiction

MICHAEL A. ARNZEN teaches horror fiction as fulltime faculty in the Writing Popular Fiction graduate program at Seton Hill University. He is a four-time winner of the Bram Stoker Award, most recently for his collection of sardonic stories and poems called *Proverbs for Monsters*. Visit Mike at www.gorelets.com, where you can get "instigation" prompts for future stories and more.

REFUSING TO LOOK AWAY

One of the most brilliant statements ever made about the horror genre was a passing remark Robert Bloch once said in an interview. I quote it often, as it has become my mantra as horror writer.

"Horror is the removal of masks."

What makes this brilliant? It goes against what most people assume. Ours is the genre most associated with the Halloween holiday, where everyone dons costumes to creep out the neighbors. Our genre, moreover, is persistently defined by shock cinema, with its never-ending series of masked slashers and costumed crazies. Too many casual fans associate our genre with the featureless plastic of the masked goalie (Jason Vorhees) or the overly-painted face of the clown (Pennywise) or the shuddersome posture of a maniac behind rigid plastic (Michael Meyers). And so many horror monsters are composed of so much plastic costuming. Horror is a genre all about the mask, but what Bloch's comment suggests is that it is the act of *removing* these coverings that horrifies us most of all.

Perhaps Bloch is pointing to what the mask ultimately suggests in its own subtle way: that something else, something other, something scary always lurks behind appearances. That all reality is superficial. And that the primary goal of horror is to lift the mask off and show us what we may not want to see behind it.

The truth is, horror both screens and reveals, covers and uncovers. It invites us to peek at "the shape under the sheet"—Stephen King's also-brilliant metaphor for the genre, described in his introduction to *Night Shift*. Beneath the mortuary shroud, death always awaits. A horror writer, King says, "takes your hand and he enfolds it in his own, and he takes you into the room and he puts your hands on the shape under the sheet...and tells you to touch it here...here...and *here*..."

It is not simply the case that horror tears the sheet off the body of fear like some magician yanking a tablecloth away from a table and leaving behind the candelabra. Though it often can and often does revel in the thrilling surprise and disturbing shock of the *suddenly revealed*, it is more often the case that horror's power lies in seduction: it seduces us into looking at things that we otherwise wish would remain enshrouded in mystery (the unknown). It probes into the places where society tells us we should not go (the taboo). Our fear is balanced against the pleasure inherent to rebelling against the rules; we thrill at doing something our parents and priests and pundits tell us we should not do. We know we shouldn't, but we "go there" anyway.

Another way of thinking about this is that horror is a striptease of suspense. It is an inherently exhibitionist genre, as much as it is the genre of fear. And this may very well be why horror gets a bum rap from the literati: horror can make a reader feel dirty, because it refuses to obey the inner sensor that tells us that such-and-such is morally wrong, that such-

and-such is ugly or grotesque, that such-and-such is perverse or unhealthy, that such-and-such is unreasonable or irrational, that such-and-such is dangerous or inhumane. Horror writers seek truth in the darkness. They remove the mask, to peer unabashedly at what it hides, horrendous warts and all.

I don't think I'm over-romanticizing the horror writer's mission when I suggest that we are explorers of the unknown, who go where others fear to tread. In our minds and in our words, anyway. Readers instinctively enjoy the "peek-a-boo" striptease of horror. When they crack open a horror book, they are receptive to being scared, like being strapped into a cart at the funhouse, ready to ride. But what that really means is that they are simply open-minded, receptive to new ideas, ready to be taken into the darkness. Earning the reader's trust is imperative. This is why King mentions how the writer "enfolds [the reader's] hand in his own": we are the tour guides to Terror Island. The characters might die in a cautionary tale, or they might discover some secret that the world needs to pay attention to. But it matters not, because our mission in taking the journey into the unknown the first place is the same: to get at the truth. The unblinking truth behind the mask.

If you wish to write horror stories, it is imperative that you understand this aesthetic. There are no "rules," really, because readers only expect the unexpected when they pick up a work of horror. In place of rules, we just have a worldview that says: "Readers peek between their fingers. I refuse to look away." We remove the mask.

The horror writer is the spotlight operator at the striptease show, true, but there is more to it than that. We are in control of what readers see and imagine, but it takes a degree of letting go of all control to set the stage in the first place. When we write our first draft, we are exploring the dark caverns of our mind, removing the censor that would stop us from "going there." Revision—literally, "re-seeing"—is daring to look at what we've unmasked *again*, and seeing if there is yet another mask still left to remove. This is perhaps even more difficult, because when we revise we are also readers. We may discover things we wish to "mask" in our own writing—secrets and confessions of our own desires that we would never reveal in everyday life. If this happens to you, think twice before you edit it out: if it makes us uncomfortable, we may be on to something good.

Ultimately, you're safe because it's all fiction. I do not have the answers or the rules, but I do know from experience that trying to craft good horror stories means trying to be honest with my readers in my quest for touching on some form of truth, even in my most radically weird fantasies or comedic gross-outs. Good horror writing is imaginative because it goes into territories that are fresh and original. The difficulty of doing this well, often is a two-sided hurdle: on the one hand, one must be truly able to "let go" and allow your unconscious mind to reveal its fears and desires; on the other, once a draft is done, the complexity of knowing what on earth to edit (ergo "censor") during revision presents itself. As to the first problem, it helps if you can write your first draft in something akin to a "hypnagogic" or "dream state." I'm not saying that you need to take illicit substances, but that your mission is to fantasize and imagine—to be "in the story world" rather than "in the real world." The problem here is that the inner censor is omnipresent (we call that a "conscience") and it is difficult to silence it. My advice here is don't silence it... argue with it. Challenge it. Make it defend itself. And give yourself freedom to play. Go hog wild and get as weird as you want. You can edit it later.

As for the second problem, how *do* we make choices about what to show our readers? How do we know what to cut? How far do we turn up the sheet? What will readers think of us if we go too far? Ultimately, you're safe because it's all fiction. You can do whatever you want and "getting away with it" may very well be the grandest of all rewards for the horror writer. But I remind you that you have to earn the reader's trust. You don't do that by being a social daredevil or a wacko who does crazy things and writes about them from experience. You do that by manipulating the elements of fiction with more care than most people do. Readers trust us to have a good story to tell, and to tell it well. But at the same time they also trust us to "go there" and (usually) bring them back afterward, changed by experience.

THE COSTUME & THE CHOREOGRAPHY

If horror is a seduction, a striptease, a game of peek-a-boo, then the way that our stories dance is our craft. Two elements of that dance are the costume (what the reader "sees"—the scenes of fiction) and the choreography (how those scenes are organized).

The two work hand-in-hand, but let me first explain something important about scene. One of the great truisms of fiction writing is the dogma that one should "show, don't tell." What this means, ultimately, is that the writing should be invisible, that the story should come to life seemingly of its own accord, and that the writer needs to be out of the picture as much as possible. Good writers craft scenes by using language that gets readers imagining things. We accomplish this by appealing to the reader's senses.

Obviously, writers use language to paint the senses, and I would advise you to think poetically: smartly employ metaphors and pay attention to the way words sound when they roll off the tongue. Words are like musical notes, so be sure to think about how the notes you are choosing are orchestrating the dance of the story. The more "other-worldly" the moment of your story, perhaps the more "poetic" your prose should become in trying to express the inexpressible.

"Imagery" is the literary term for an appeal to the reader's senses, but it does not only mean to draw "word pictures" that appear in the mind like a visual image. In addition to sight, one shouldn't forget the other four senses (taste, touch, sound and smell), but it is true that in horror fiction the senses of sight and sound seem dominant (just as they are dominant in the movies). All five senses are the palette from which we paint our scenes; we do not necessarily use all five all the time, but it is important to choose our colors carefully.

Beyond image-rich language, the best way to work that palette is to put yourself literally into the sensorium of your main character, and to think about how that character would actually perceive the reality of any given situation. Thus, you choreograph the scene by following the *natural* way we use our senses to apprehend the world, even if we are writing about something supernatural. For example, if your protagonist is entering a room where there is a rotting undead corpse under the bed, it would be more appropriate to begin that scene with an appeal to the sense of smell rather than catching a glimpse of some slimy trail on the floor leading toward the bed. Although we see it all the time on TV and in the movies, the reality of death is an experience that society actually works very hard to cover up (with the secrecy of the morgue, the antiseptics of detergents, the makeup of the mortician), so the smell of it, especially, is not a familiar one to most people. The odor would catch the protagonist's attention long before they had any motivation to look toward the floor. And perhaps they wouldn't even do *that* until they felt their shoes slide on something wet and viscous beneath them on the hardwood. Then—understanding the need to be cautious—they might stop, look, and listen—not like a kid on a sidewalk, but like an animal detecting a predator nearby. Their sensorium would go on alert. They'd see nothing, but suddenly hear something breathing heavy and smacking its lips...something below them...something beneath the bed...where black blood seems to trail, painting the wood like the brushstroke of some drunken mad giant...

The rookie horror writer would race through this sort of scene by describing what the protagonist sees after entering the room. Eyes are like pointers, but too often they dart around cartoonishly in horror fiction: they survey the visual realm, rapidly presenting an itemized list of details. There's nothing wrong with using the visual plane to "show" a reader what a room might look like, but when you can put your reader into the character's head as they try to make sense of their environment, it works much better because the reader will vicariously live the experience on their own. The writer gets in the way when they simply "list" the items in, say a bedroom, because they are arbitrarily choosing what items to describe—a candlestick here, a photograph there, a nightstand over there. The random decisions call attention to a writer trying to stage the scene. But the method I have described above works better because it has a sense of direction that entirely depends on the character's concern (e.g. conflict) as well as the limitations of their viewpoint, *moving from uncertainty toward certainty*, even if that certainty is yet another mystery. And even though the character never sees what is under the bed, they are certain that something dangerous lurks there, smacking its lips despite the obvious trail of blood, signaling death.

If horror is the removal of masks, then what I have already described has been only a suspenseful build-up to a revelation of what is actually going on under the bed. This is where writers have to make a choice. Either they hold back and let the reader imagine for themselves (usually drawing this imaginary image from the details you've given—like the smacking of lips and the trail of blood) or they get down on their hands and knees and shine a spotlight on the source of all those crazy clues. Assuming you have built up the reader's curiosity well, swelling them up to the bursting point, you now have to deliver. You must choose between subtlety and garish shock—between letting the mask slip down a peg, or tearing it full force away from the face altogether.

Some might argue that "not showing" is the dignified choice, because it allows the reader to imagine what might be, which is preferable because readers will "fill in the blanks" with their own nightmares, rather than having their noses rubbed in whatever proverbial crap the writer wants to show them.

But I would counter that all of this has been striptease, and that neither choice matters so long as the writer is not simply "teasing" but is actually revealing something concrete to the senses and the build-up of tension is finally released in a rewarding way. The final garment needs to be torn asunder, and whether we are shown a tasteful set of tassels or a pulsing purple object matters very little. Either outcome will be applauded by the audience, if the dance has been a satisfying one, and the reader is rewarded with surprise.

There are limits to this metaphor. In a real striptease, the lighting is garish. In horror fiction, the lighting should progressively get darker. Darkness is symbolic of death, but also seasons and hours. It is always darkest before the dawn, and time-wise, the chronicle of your scene should dim darker and darker. I am not saying that all horror stories should take place at the "witching hour," but think of lighting as a pigment in your imagery: choose the darker colors as things progress. The darker things are, the more our pupils dilate, and the more we actively try to see. It is ironic that when we are most in shadows, our bodies are actually seeing the most—it is just that we are seeing more blackness. Our eyes panic in the darkness, and are most concerned with the edges of the shadows. That is where the striptease of terror takes place: on the edge between what we see and can't see, between our need to see more and our desire to see less.

We all wear masks of flesh and—just like the ring around the camera lens—our range of vision is always limited to the sockets that surround our eyes. Craft your scenes to dance along that edge and you'll disturb your reader in the most satisfying of ways. There are things that we cannot see in the places beyond. Your job, simply, is to *go there*.

CHAPTER 11

Jonathan Maberry

Fight and Action Scenes In Horror

JONATHAN MABERRY is the multiple Bram Stoker Award-winning author of novels *Patient Zero, Ghost Road Blues,* etc., nonfiction books *Zombie CSU, The Cryptopedia,* etc., comics *Punisher: Naked Kill* and *Wolverine: Ghosts,* and over 1100 magazine articles. Jonathan is the co-creator (with Laura Schrock) of *On the Slab,* an entertainment news show for ABC Disney / Stage 9, to be released on the Internet in 2009. He is a Contributing Editor for *The Big Thrill* (the newsletter of the International Thriller Writers), and is a member of SFWA, MWA and HWA. Visit his website at www.jonathanmaberry.com or on Facebook and MySpace.

Everybody loves a good fight scene.

Whether it's a road-weary Indiana Jones pulling a pistol and shooting that big guy with the sword; or Ellen Ripley strapping on a power loader and going toe-to-toe with the alien queen; or Buffy kicking some vampire ass. We love fight scenes, especially in fantastic fiction.

But I'm a purist. Both as a reader and a writer I like my fantasy to be as believable as possible. I'll accept that there are werewolves if I'm reading a werewolf story, but if a puny Casper Milquetoast decks a werewolf with a single punch then I'm bailing on the story. Conversely, if a vampire backhands Van Helsing and sends him flying twenty feet into a brick wall… and Van Helsing *gets up* again, I'm out of there. The first is unlikely, the latter is improbable. And fight scenes, no matter what the genre, are all about what *is* possible.

This is particularly true in horror because we're already asking so much of the reader. Horror stories are about creating a scenario in which something horrific is presented in such a way that readers are willing to suspend their disbelief. We want them to accept the possibility of a werewolf or a demon or vampire. We want readers to buy into the reality of humans pitted against something supernatural—or unnatural. It's asking a lot of the reader to accept the fantastic, so if they grant us that license we can't abuse them for it. It's a matter of artistic integrity. It's a matter of fairness. And it's also a matter of basic honest storytelling.

An action scene in horror can take many forms. It can be a fight between a human and a mad killer. It can be a struggle between a human and a monster. It can be a struggle between two monsters. The core element is the struggle itself—the fight scene, and a good fight scene has to be based on what is—and is not—possible.

Fighting is about attack and defense. Even in the real world there are very few 'fair fights'. Everything comes down to variables. For example, you can have a boxing match between two heavyweight contenders and it will never be precisely even. One will be heavier, and those extra pounds could be in the form of muscle or fat or even denser bones. The extra weight lends mass to a punch but it also requires more effort to move. On the other hand one of the boxers will likely have slightly longer reach, and though this allows him to strike from a greater distance, longer arms don't block or parry as efficiently as shorter arms. Larger feet provide more square inches of stability but they are inherently clumsier.

In all fights the variables provide advantages and disadvantages.

Everything matters in a fight. You have physical specifics to consider: height, general fitness, weight, muscle-to-fat ratios, limb length, bone and muscle density, pain threshold, pre-existing injuries, natural and acquired reflexes, the presence of medical conditions, allergies, eyesight, and so on. Any one of these factors could give someone an edge or become a liability.

Then you have the physical environment. The type of surface (a fight on a sandy beach is far different than a fight on a flight of stone stairs), available space, temperature, available light, and access to objects useful as defensive or offensive weapons. The personal experience of the combatants matters. Previous fight experience, experience with sports and sports injuries, previous training in any aspect of fighting, courage, emotions, and psychology are all factors.

Even if a person has been trained as a fighter there are variables. Ten years practicing Tai Chi is less likely to help someone win a fight than one year of goju karate. Someone who is a judo champion may not be able to win against someone who has spent a year in Special Forces.

And intention matters. Most people have never fought for their lives. Even someone who has been in a dozen barroom brawls may not have what it takes to fight to the death. Some fighters are so thoroughly committed to the conflict that they will do anything to win; others are governed by factors like timidity, honor, restraint, or compassion. A person fending off a violent attack by a mugger may be able to summon enough outrage to do great bodily harm; but that same person fending off a violent attack by a hysterical or psychologically unbalanced loved one may not be able to bring themselves to harm the other person at all.

So…what's all this have to do with horror stories?

Horror stories, no matter how fantastical, are distortions of the real world. A vampire hunter squaring off against a hungry bloodsucker is not all that dissimilar to a small woman trying to defeat an enraged and muscular male rapist. The differences in size, the presence of violent intentions, the certainty of a committed aggression by a more powerful enemy *define* the situation. We have to start with what we know of the combatants and then build the most logical possible scene around that.

What do we know about the vampire? If we take the standard pop culture view, then the vampire is immortal, it is considerably stronger than a human being, it's faster than a human, it can withstand virtually any ordinary injury, it doesn't breathe, it doesn't bleed in any useful way, and it's very hard to kill. Its weaknesses are few, but they are there: the vampire fears holy objects, can't abide sunlight, is repulsed by garlic, and will die if beheaded, set ablaze or pierced through the heart with wood.

In good horror stories the vampire hunter comes prepared to this encounter as often as possible. Hammer, stake, garlic, cross. Maybe a torch and an axe. The tension of the scene will generally be built around a series of attempts to do things the right way and then the introduction of complications that spoil the easy fix, and finally a desperate struggle against seemingly impossible odds. All good in theory, but also potentially very trite.

Yes, a really smart vampire hunter would show up an hour after dawn with a bulldozer and knock down the castle walls; or indulge in some creative arson; or if they want to do it in a more hands-on fashion they'd eat a pound of garlic, smear garlic oil all over themselves, sew crosses onto every square inch of their clothing, and show up with sixty or seventy very close friends all of whom have axes, stakes and torches. But that would make for a very short vampire tale. So, to build a scene in which tension and suspense are allowed to develop, the vampire hunter encounters a series of unfortunate incidents that prevent him from getting to the vampire's lair until sunset. Now it's a race against time (and that's always a good thing). Maybe the vampire has captured a loved one who will die if not rescued right away. More tension. When the vampire hunter opens the coffin...the vampire isn't there.

Crap. Turns out the vampire doesn't sleep in a coffin and uses the traditional folklore as a dodge to fool would be vampire hunters. Now the vampire hunter is face to face with a monster that is, as we've established, stronger and faster and hard to kill. As dire as the situation has become it's not game over. This is when we get to the good stuff. This is when we have to solve problems by looking at the combatants and then build a scene in which the hero wins because he does something *possible*. It can be weird, daring, even unlikely, but it has to be possible…and it can never be a cheat. No *deus ex machina* in the form of a pointy piece of furniture onto which the vampire trips and falls.

When writing my Pine Deep Trilogy—*Ghost Road Blues, Dead Man's Song,* and *Bad Moon Rising* (Pinnacle Books, 2006, '07 and '08) I wanted to create a story in which real people without superpowers encountered vampires. I knew from the beginning that I wanted the fight scenes to reflect my own views and experiences as a long time practitioner of jujutsu and teacher of self-defense. And I wanted the encounters with the vampires to be frightening and exciting.

In the first novel, *Ghost Road Blues,* the first major fight scene is between two humans. One is an ex-cop named Malcolm Crow, who is short, thin and unimposing; but he has a number of years invested in the martial arts. The other character is Karl Ruger, a psychotic killer known for his ruthlessness and violence. If this was the kind of thing people could bet on, the hot money would be on Ruger because he's bigger, stronger, and crazy. On the other hand, Ruger also believes that his winning is a foregone conclusion.

When Crow first encounters Ruger, the killer is strangling Crow's girlfriend Val, on the lawn outside of her farmhouse. It's dark and a storm is tearing apart the heavens. Ruger uses Val as a shield to get close enough to sucker Crow, but Crow slips the sucker punch. The ensuing fight includes some of the nastiest stuff two people can do to each another. Crow wins the fight, but just barely.

The tension in the scene begins when Crow realizes that he's up against a legendary psychopath. The immediate threat to Val dials up his personal stake; otherwise he might have retreated to safe distance and called for help. She has to be saved right now. The slow burn to the sucker-punch builds into the potential for Crow, or his girlfriend, or both of them, to be killed. It's an ensemble cast, which means no one is entirely safe.

The tension is tweaked when the sucker-punch fails and Crow turns the table on Ruger. Then it's turned back around when Ruger proves to be far tougher than anyone Crow has ever fought. On the other hand Ruger's overconfidence creates a fragment of opportunity for Crow, and he rides that to a victory.

At the end of the scene both men are battered nearly insensate. The blows given and received have damaged them. They can't just shake it off. They're exhausted, hurt, stressed, and worn down.

Then, after Ruger is down, Crow makes the mistake of leaving him to go and check on Val. Ruger is able to recover the gun Crow dropped during the sucker-punch just as cops arrive on the scene. Ruger opens fire and shoots the cop; Crow manages to get the cop's gun and returns fire. They both fall in a hail of bullets.

The scene's foundation is the suspense of when these two players will finally encounter each other, and if Crow will get to Val's farm in time to save her. It's twisted by the tactics during the fight, and made real by the accuracy of the techniques used by each man. No one does anything absurd—no double spinning Ninja death kicks. No punching a guy ten times in the face without breaking a hand.

Near the end of the book Crow encounters Ruger again. The killer is different now...he's becoming something supernatural. Crow doesn't even know he's in a supernatural story, and the shock he experiences at Ruger's unnatural speed and strength nearly results in his death. This new version of Ruger is far too strong for him to defeat in unarmed combat. And he doesn't. Luckily Val comes to the rescue with a handgun from another cop Ruger has brutalized; and Crow grabs the cop's throwdown piece, and together they pour a lot of lead into Ruger, who goes down.

Even then Crow isn't sure that the killer is dead.

He's right to be concerned.

By the second book, *Dead Man's Song,* Crow has become convinced that something supernatural is happening, and though he doesn't encounter Ruger in that book, we see the killer moving behind the scenes, helping to create an army of vampires. Bad times are coming, and the whole story is built on the expectation of what *might* be coming.

In the final book, *Bad Moon Rising,* Crow confronts Ruger twice. The first time Ruger tries to lay a trap for Crow, but by now Crow is hip to the fact that the killer is a vampire. Crow escapes that threat by bringing something else to the party: smarts. Since he knows he can't possibly defeat a vampire *mano-a-mano,* he slathers himself with garlic and injects garlic oil into the shells in his shotgun. When Ruger sees the effect of the garlic on one of his vampire henchmen, he flees.

In this case the threat the hero faces has increased—as all threats in horror fiction should—and Crow goes to the next level. He uses brains when brawn alone just won't work. We all know that—at some point—Crow and Ruger are going to have a final smackdown, but with each of them raising the stakes we no longer know exactly what that will look like. The uncertainty amplifies tension and satisfies the need of the reader to be surprised as well as entertained.

In the final battle, Crow and a dwindling handful of his friends, try to stop the army of vampires from resurrecting a far more powerful creature that will, for all intents and purposes, become a vampire god. Crow believes that he's going to die in this battle. He's already seen several of his friends fall—including characters who have been key players from the beginning. This, by the way, is a great way of keeping the readers on the edge of their seat: if we create believable characters and present them in situations through which the reader becomes emotionally invested…and then *kill them off,* we're serving up tension all the way to the end of the book. In good fiction no one is safe.

When Crow faces Ruger for the last time, Crow has his weapons: a bug-sprayer unit filled with gasoline and a lighter, guns with garlic enhanced bullets, and a samurai sword whose blade is coated with garlic. Through one mischance after another Crow's weapons are taken away from him. Now that we've established that brains can defeat supernatural strength, we need to take that advantage away from the hero. It ultimately comes down to a fight more closely resembling their first encounter. Crow wins because, even now Ruger is confident that his own victory is a foregone conclusion; and because Crow is resourceful and practical.

Good horror requires that action be grounded in possibility. It demands that conflict and complications lay the groundwork for tension. And it absolutely needs suspense to be the driving force rather than shock. Readers are smart, experienced, and devoted…and if they are willing to suspend their disbelief long enough for us to tell our tale, then we owe it to them to make them glad they did.

CHAPTER 12

Tom Piccirilli

Exploring Personal Themes

TOM PICCIRILLI lives in Colorado where, besides writing, he spends an inordinate amount of time watching trash cult films and reading Gold Medal classic noir and hardboiled novels. He's a fan of Asian cinema, especially horror movies, pinky violence, and samurai flicks. He also likes walking his dogs around the neighborhood. Are you starting to get the hint that he doesn't have a particularly active social life? Well to heck with you, buddy, yours isn't much better. Give him any static and he'll smack you in the mush, dig? Tom also enjoys making new friends. He's the author of twenty novels including *Shadow Season, The Cold Spot, The Coldest Mile, The Midnight Road*, and *A Choir of Ill Children*. He's a four-time winner of the Bram Stoker Award, winner of the International Thriller Writers Award, and has been a final nominee for the World Fantasy Award and the Edgar Award. Learn more at www.thecoldspot.blogspot.com.

Let's talk about "theme" for a bit.

The concept of themes found in fiction has understandably gotten a hard knock in the horror field. After all, it's the sort of thing you're supposed to hunt around for when you're reading some dry academic paper on the "underlying homosexual imagery in Mary Shelley's *Frankenstein*" or "The abstraction of Historical Evil found in Stephen King's *The Shining*." It's the kind of stuff that steals the flavor out of our very favorite pieces of literature.

By the way, I wrote both of those papers back in college.

Also, is it actually possible to write about the so-called larger world themes in horror? Aren't we supposed to be dealing with simple entertainment concerning fear, suspense and action?

Well, yes and no. Of course you're supposed to tell a good story first and foremost, but that doesn't mean you can't try to explore issues and topics you feel are especially important to you. Specific themes and images that recur in your stories are there either through personal interest or because you want to use them as a memorable signature of sorts, a stamp that marks the work as your own.

You may not even know they're there.

Offbeat novelist Harry Crews always features what are proclaimed to be "freaks" in his work. Yet he swears that his wife had to point out the fact to him that his first three books feature midgets before he realized he was writing so prominently about them. Crews himself suffered from childhood paralysis in impoverished Bacon County, Georgia and was so emotionally scarred by the experience of having strangers staring at his crooked legs as a child that—even though he eventually recovered—he's always felt physically freakish since that time.

Finding what incites your emotions, your sense of resolve, and weaving them into motifs and sub-text can be cathartic for the author. Stephen King once said that he felt he was one of the sanest people he knew because he managed to put every frustration, anxiety and phobia he had down on the page, and in the process managed to exorcise those problems. In our fiction we can address whatever personal or social ills we perceive, whatever major arguments and questions we might have about the world. We can route out the most significant feelings and apply them time and again.

But of course, conveying the substance of this through our fiction can be a double-edged sword. There's always a chance you'll wind up on a soapbox without meaning to. There's also the possibility that you'll tend to repeat yourself, and that the subject matter itself will hamper your imagination and force issues to the forefront that aren't necessarily best for the story you're trying to tell.

So when are you going too far and why should you worry about it in the first place?

Well, you probably shouldn't. You should simply be aware of the issues that might be hidden between the lines of your work. Thematic plot threads, symbolism, and recurring motifs are simply other means to an end: making your fiction as strong as it can be.

To put a personal spin on it: My father died when I was quite young and I've explored the idea of fathers quite frequently in my writing. Father figures are either long dead, forlorn, or tragic personages. This isn't a reflection on my father so much as it has become an odd focus of my storytelling. I find value, edge, and atmosphere in investigating that area of my sensibility. That particular figure used to that particular purpose holds some resonance for me as an author, and inspires me onwards.

Religion fascinates and disturbs me, and I often impart this in my work through the subject matter. I tend to fuse elements of my Catholic upbringing with research I've done on other religions and the occult. Recurrence of this sort is to be expected throughout an author's career. We gravitate to that which enthralls us.

It's also true I have what I call my "water stories." Since I grew up on Long Island and spent a lot of time at the beach. The vastness of the ocean is a powerful concept, beneath the waves in all that darkness. It sparks a great many ideas for me, a lot of primal urges and awe and panic which I can use in my writing.

Almost everyone will find their own natural signature concepts and images that provide the themes for their work over the courses of their careers. I think it's important, though not necessary, to have something that you can use as a seal or mark to make your fiction stand out. These are underlying messages that the reader will pick up on.

Edgar Allan Poe repeatedly returned to the notion of the premature burial. Crime writer Charles Williams' novels are filled with skippers and boats, based on his seaman's background. Ed Gorman uses the recurring story lines of quaint innocent American backwoods towns often hide the darkest, most vicious secrets. British horror author Simon Clark often uses the end of the world motif as a narrative chiller, exploring mankind's dissolution and redemption. John Irving uses themes that revolve around abnormal families, children in danger, and the recurrent symbols of bears, private schools, and wrestling. As mentioned, Harry Crews uses the physically grotesque and freakish. These topics and emblems make the work immediately identifiable with the author.

CHAPTER 13

Mort Castle

New Fiction Blend: History, Fantasy, Horror

MORT CASTLE has four decades of writing experience, which equals about 600+ publications ... or "I'm not prolific, just old." He edited the essential horror-scribe reference works *Writing Horror* and *On Writing Horror*, contributes regularly to *The Writer* and *Writer's Digest*, and teaches writing at Columbia College Chicago. Among his honors: Castle is the only living writer with stories in all five of J.N. Williamson's acclaimed *Masques* anthologies; he's been cited as one of "21 Leaders in the Arts for the 21st Century in Chicago," and his novel *Strangers* in its Polish translation, *Obcy*, made the "10 Best Horror-Thriller Novels of 2008" in *Newsweek Polska*. Castle edits *Doorways Magazine* and has two or three new books coming out this year, some of them in English.

An Intro to Outré

"History + Fiction" has been a viable formula since *The Histories of Herodotus of Halicarnassus*, circa 440 BC, with which work the author earned himself not only the sobriquet "Father of History" but "The Father of Lies." Today, a unique cross-genre blend of history and fantastic fiction is exciting authors and enticing readers.

The new modus operandi is "History + Horror" or "History + Fantasy," or, if you're into literary trends, you might say, "History + Magical Realism." (Magical Realism: a literary genre presenting a credible cosmos in which all sorts of bizarre stuff happens without being thought anymore unusual than the bizarre events on the nightly news.)

Some classify this "new" category as *Slipstream;* one of its finest authors, Rudy Rucker (the elder), favors the term "Transrealistic Fiction." I'd call it "outré fiction," if I were sure I was pronouncing it right. Whatever the label, it's a uniquely contemporary melding of "anything *can* happen" with "what *did* happen."

For example: Stephen Marlowe's novel *Lighthouse at the End of the World*, gives us Edgar Allan Poe's last five days on this and alternative other Earths—and in C. Auguste Dupin's Paris, on a tropic island, and at that lonely lighthouse at the end ...

Steve Savile presents *Houdini's Last Illusion*, a novella in which the master magician sees ghostly dead magicians and decides his demise is near.

My own story, "Buckeye Jim in Egypt" (in the collection *Moon on The Water*: banjo playing title character visits Southern Illinois in 1929, witnesses the execution of gangster Charlie Birger, the state's last legal hanging, and reveals himself as the "Widow's Son," resurrected by Jesus and fated to live until the Messiah's Second Coming.

By using recorded fact as story basis or background, the fictionist gains an immediate advantage. Fiction needs credibility. The reader must be able to say, "Yes, given these circumstances, this could really happen." We do *not* want to hear, "Ah, it's just a story"; that comes from a reader who's likewise saying, "So who cares? Just something someone made up... "

As genres, horror and fantasy possess a built-in liability: *21st Century sophisticates know people die of* cancer, *not* curses, *know that black widow spiders, roadside bombs, and rabid Rottweillers can kill, but not werewolves, vampires, or ghosts.* It's a struggle, making credible that which is patently *incred-*

ible.

But when we *start* with historical event(s), such as:

A) - The brief, intense life of free-thinker, poet, and libertine George Gordon Lord Byron (1788 - 1824) ...

B) - The suspicious death of President Warren G. Harding, just prior to the revelation of the Teapot Dome scandal ...

C) - The Great Fire of London of 1666, which destroyed most of the city ...

Then our reader knows there's a *reality root*; it is the rare reader who will fail to suspend disbelief to grant you a fantasy license—*once you have established the reality*.

To go weird-working from the above historical examples:

A) - ... so *that* explains how Lord Byron became a vampire ... *Lord of the Dead*, (1995), a novel by Tom Holland.

B) - Harding did not kill himself and his wife didn't murder him. Novelist Glen David Gold's explanation of "what's up with Harding?" can be found in *Carter Beats the Devil* (2001).

C) - Historians theorize London's blaze started with a bakery "fire-box door left askance": I postulate that a teenage "fire witch" magically con-figured the conflagration in my novella "Hotties," from my story collection *Nations of the Living, Nations of the Dead* (2002).

TO BEND HISTORY ITSELF: YOUR HISTORICAL PREMISE

Those of us forced to endure boring history lessons in school know that mere chronologies and geographies provide no inherent interest.

The historical incident that clicks with us writers is one that allows us to focus on the ageless and endlessly fascinating subject, *Ye Olde Human Condition*—while also setting our imaginations a'spin:

July 24, 1915: the passenger loaded excursion ship *The East-*

land capsized at the dock in the Chicago River; 850 people died.

That's a historical note—but here's the *human* note that grabbed this writer:

> Charles R. E. Bowles, a 17 year old superb swimmer, dove again and again into the oily river, bringing up the bodies of at least 40 victims and earning himself the nickname "The Human Frog." One dive retrieved two bodies: a mother clasping her baby to her breast.

My story in progress, for obvious reasons entitled "The Human Frog," deals with the rough vagabond life the adult Charles Bowles led, haunted by the ghosts of the 40 dead and the words they spoke as he brought them from the murky water.

Heroism and haunting allow me to explore the theme succinctly stated by Clare Boothe Luce, "No good deed goes unpunished."

Surveying any historical period, your research will give you little, not so little, and really big "how about that!" nuggets that will prime your story making engines:

> The Etruscans invented false teeth around 700 BC. Joseph Bramah of England crafted the supposedly burglar-proof "padlock" in 1786. In 1920 Thomas A. Edison told a reporter he was developing a device to contact the spirits of the dead.

Now, you need to discover such historical springboards for your own stories ...

RESEARCH THE FACTS—OR OPTION TWO

Books, educational courses, and entire academic disciplines have focused on the methodology and goals of research. Your goal as a fiction writer is finding history you can use. Techniques... Well, in an article of this length, I can share with you only a few of the strategies and sources that work for me.

The Internet has become a researcher's first resource—and, like everybody else, my search engine of choice is "Google." The Net also helps us develop our discriminatory powers: *What is fact and what is the schizoid blathering of a cybernut?*

Before the Web, people had an easily accessed info-source called *books*. We still do. The print encyclopedia, though generalist and inclusive, usually yields greater in-depth coverage on any given topic than the typical website.

I'll limit my book suggestions to a few I've found particularly valuable, and naturally some of these deal with those epochs that intrigue me. Your mindset will vary:

The People's Almanac series edited by any one or more of the Wallace Family, Irving, Amy, and David Wallechinsky, offers thousands of "Strange but true!" anecdotes and vignettes. Out of print, these books are readily found in libraries and garage sales. I particularly like *The People's Almanac Presents the Twentieth Century: History with the Boring Bits Left Out.*

A more recent series can be viewed as a literary descendent of *People's* books: the "Uncle John" bathroom readers, among them *Uncle John's Bathroom Reader Plunges into History* and *Uncle John's Bathroom Reader Extraordinary Book of Facts And Bizarre Information*. Once you get past the potty humor, these reference works offer oddities you won't find in *The Decline and Fall of Anybody's Empire.*

For facts *and* often pictures to help me understand those facts, the children's section of the library is the place to go. To learn what a chimney sweep's "mum" might serve for breakfast or how many hours in the pillory a Pilgrim might spend for fishing on Sunday, the books Walter Hazen has done in the "Everyday Life" series for Good Year Books (*Ancient Times, Revolutionary War, The Great Depression,* and many, many more!) are particularly useful. They are filled with photographs and illustrations and, targeted as they are for grades four - eight, seldom confused me.

You can seek and meet living witnesses to the history you plan to fanta-fictionalize (if it's relatively recent history) or individuals who've acquired specialized historical expertise in everything from Roman toga draping for the full figure to German dueling society etiquette for left-handed swordsmen. When I was researching my above mentioned "Buckeye Jim" story, I talked with one man who'd been at Charlie Birger's jail house courtyard hanging and another who used to drop in and chat with the genial gangster at Shady Rest, the roadhouse Birger owned in Harrisburg, Illinois (which was, not at all coincidentally, the site of the first aerial bombing with the borders of the USA).

Finally, advice you won't hear in grad school. Consider Andy Warhol's dictum: "Art is what you can get away with." So are (ahem) the facts, as anyone who follows politics will attest. Facts are important for your story ... so be sure to make up good ones.

Remember Edison's "talk to the dead" gadget? J.N. Williamson, the late horror writer, added a "soft fact," plausible enough that we grant it *could have happened* status: *Edison's device worked.* That's the premise of Williamson's 1991 novel *Horror House* in which Edison's gizmo speaks with the dead in contemporary times: the *evil* dead.

With *what was* meeting *what if?* fiction, you can plant your feet solidly in the known world—and set your mind free to voyage beyond the stars, beyond dimensions, beyond all we know or *think* we know.

And you'll take your reader with you.

CHAPTER 14

Jeff Strand

Adding Humor to Your Horror

JEFF STRAND is the author of such horror/comedy novels as *Graverobbers Wanted (No Experience Necessary)*, *The Sinister Mr. Corpse*, and *Benjamin's Parasite*. He's also the Bram Stoker Award-nominated author of a "serious" novel, *Pressure*. His Gleefully Macabre website is conveniently located at www.jeffstrand.com.

Let's talk about dead babies.

In real life, there aren't many things more tragic than a dead baby. But if you grab any random ten-year-old off the street (you probably shouldn't), more likely than not they'll be able to entertain you with delightful jokes about infants floating face-down in a bathtub, being dismembered, resorting to cannibalism to escape dump trucks, and suffering other gruesome fates...the grosser the better.

Though losing a child is a fate you wouldn't wish on any mother, the fact is that dead babies are an *excellent* source of comedy, especially when their eyeballs have been poked out. And it's not just dead babies. A doctor delivering the news that you have only two weeks left to live (and that's the good news!), a skydiver's parachute not opening, somebody's arm popping off at an inopportune time, and a rabid dog mauling an elderly woman are all perfectly acceptable material for a joke.

Is this because, as humans, we find it difficult to cope with or even comprehend such horrors, so we use them for comedic effect to help us better deal with them?

I dunno. Maybe, kinda. Personally, I think we're just sickos. I mean, c'mon, the college student who creates an elaborate online animation of The Puppy Blender isn't doing it as a defense mechanism. We're all warped! It's fine! Let's embrace it!

In fiction, however, humor and horror wouldn't automatically seem to be snuggly bedfellows, at least to the outside world. But while you admittedly don't see much in the way of humorous horror at novel length, I'd guess that most established horror writers have at some point written at least one tale that's meant to be funny. It's only natural. Horror writers, in general, are hilarious people. Go to a convention some time. Bring alcohol.

Some humorous horror is simply a funny tale with a horror-themed premise. Or it can be a horrific tale delivered with a wink. The story may not contain jokes, per se, and you may not actually laugh, but there's an underlying sense of fun to the proceedings. You can tell that the author was wearing a twisted little grin as he or she wrote the blood-drenched decapitation scene.

And some humorous horror uses both elements equally. You laugh, then you scream, then you laugh, then you scream. Or you laugh and scream at the same time, making this weird noise that hurts your throat and earns you strange looks from the other people in the padded room.

If you're writing horror, though, the odds are that you're not trying to write a big wacky splatter comedy—you probably just want to sprinkle occasional touches of humor in an otherwise "serious" story. There are a few reasons to do this:

Realism. Real life is funny. Real people are funny. Even people in concentration camps during World War II enjoyed their moments of levity (probably not in a goofy Roberto Benigni manner, but they did laugh sometimes). So when you add touches of believable humor to a book, it can make it more accessible to the reader and more directly connected to the real world.

Empathy. We like people who make us laugh. Of course, we probably want to laugh *with* our lead characters and not *at* them, but a couple of lines of humorous dialogue can go a long way toward making a character sympathetic and likeable to a reader. Similarly, if you put them in a funny situation that your reader can relate to, you'll gain extra empathy for your characters.

Relief of tension. A big one. If you have a heavy-duty dramatic moment or a heart-stopping scene of terror, a well-placed bit of humor can be invaluable. There's only so long that your reader can handle a high level of tension before it begins to lose its effectiveness.

For example, say I'm being mugged, and the mugger holds a gun to my head. I'm going to be pretty tense. But let's say he stands there and keeps that gun to my head for ten minutes. In the ninth minute, am I going to be as tense as I was in the first? Probably not. I'll have gotten used to the tension level. I'm not saying that I'll be all comfy and secure, of course, but the tension will have faded a bit.

But what if after five minutes the mugger lowers the gun? My tension level is greatly reduced. I can take a breath. Then the bastard suddenly presses the gun to my head again. My tension level shoots right back near the top of the charts.

Comic relief, done properly, can work the same way. A perfect example is near the end of the movie *Silence of the Lambs,* when Clarice is in Buffalo Bill's basement, trying to rescue the kidnapped girl. The scene is extremely suspenseful and nerve-wracking...and then Clarice calls out to the girl "It's okay! You're safe!" Now, the girl is anything *but* safe at this point, so this line gets a big laugh. It gives the audience a second to take a breath, and then we return to the thrilling finale. Without that tiny gap in the tension, we might not be sweating it out quite as heavily by the end of the scene.

Comic relief can simply be moments of humor the author throws in without really even thinking about it; he or she sees a spot for a touch of humor, pops it in there, and moves on.

Or maybe you want to lighten the tone. Maybe you have an agonizing scene with a mother and father losing their child, and you want to brighten the mood before your readers get completely depressed. Maybe you have an incredibly intense scene and simply need to give the reader a chance to take a breath. This is where you'd want to incorporate a well-timed moment of comic relief.

IMPORTANT RULE: Bad comic relief is always worse than no comic relief.

If it feels forced, get rid of it. Going back a few decades, you remember Wes Craven's *Last House on the Left*, don't you? This is the ultimate example of comic relief gone terribly, terribly wrong. Because the film is so disturbing, the filmmakers sought to lighten things up, in the form of a pair of idiot cops out of the worst slapstick farce imaginable. These goofy scenes are *completely* at odds with the rest of the movie. Yeah, they lighten the mood, but at the cost of the audience wondering, "*What* were they thinking?"

So, it's better to leave your readers completely depressed after that big funeral scene than to have them thinking, "What a stupid joke."

ANOTHER IMPORTANT RULE: Always be true to your characters.

When adding comic relief, always make sure that your character would really say/think/do that (or that his- or her actions are believably *out* of character). This is particularly important in a horror novel; make sure your protagonist wouldn't be too scared to say something funny!

But let's back up a bit. Where do we get these funny ideas to include in our horror fiction?

The easiest place to start, of course, is to use our own lives (our personalities, experiences, and observations) for humor fodder. Some people have made gobs of money writing about nothing *but* their own lives. But of course we're talking about fiction here, so we've got to switch things around, make them work for your particular story.

Every once in a while, you'll hear, see, or experience something that you can use as-is. It's a special gift from the Writing Gods. For example, I was visiting my in-laws, and my father-in-law was talking about how he was considering buying a descrambler to pick up satellite TV signals. My wife explained that it was illegal. My father-in-law, being completely serious, said that it *couldn't* be illegal, because satellite TV signals traveled through the air, and nobody could tell him what to do with the air on his own property.

My immediate thought: "That's going in a book."

And it did. Not only does the character of Zachary in my novel *Mandibles* have the line about the air, but I used that attitude as a major factor in developing his character. It was a comedy freebie. Unfortunately, it's usually not that easy.

So let's start by looking at ourselves. What's funny about you? Probably plenty...especially if you're a writer. Me, I have this phobia about going to get my hair cut and having the hairdresser actually want me to provide input beyond "Get rid of about an inch." That's all I want to say. I want it to be about the same, but shorter. Don't ask me about tapering or what I want blended or any of that. I recently got my hair cut and the lady wanted input on every other slice! It was nerve-wracking! When the haircut is over, I'm going to say, "Yes, it looks fine," no matter what they've done to it. And I can't figure out the mirror at the end, when you're supposed to use the hand-held mirror to look at the back of your head in the full-size mirror. I can't get the angles right. I'm so lame. I also get in trouble from my wife when I get home. "Didn't you tell them what you wanted?" "Yes! Shorter."

Now, finding funny things about yourself doesn't have to involve sounding like a complete geek. But I'm guessing that you don't have to think very hard to find these things, whether they're personality traits, speech patterns, or even the way you look. And you don't have to look for stuff that's ha-ha funny or even mild chuckle funny, just stuff that has comic potential.

It may be easier to think of funny things about your family, friends, co-workers, or even strangers. It doesn't have to be recurring traits. It could be something they said that one time. Not exactly something that's going to have the readers wetting themselves with laughter, but perhaps it's worth a minor little grin. Again, you're not necessarily looking to write an all-out horror / comedy, just adding a bit of levity.

Try it one day. When you wake up in the morning, decide that you're going to pay attention to all of the funny things that happen around you. Oh, what the heck? Try it tomorrow. You don't have to write them down, but just be observant. Again, they don't have to be those uproarious moments that cause you to shoot beverages through your nose, just anything that causes you to smile.

Okay, to illustrate adding comic relief to an otherwise serious piece of work, here's the opening of my novel *Pressure* with the humor eliminated:

> For a while, the bullets were the only things keeping me alive.
>
> It was a sack of one hundred and fourteen of them, each with a date scratched onto the casing. The first date was nearly four months ago, a Thursday. I'd spent that entire morning in my bathtub, tears streaming down my face, the barrel of a revolver in my

mouth. I wasn't sure that I really wanted to commit suicide, but yet I couldn't force myself to pry the gun barrel from between my teeth.

Finally I did pull the gun away and removed the bullet. And then I scratched 12/25 onto the casing with a pocketknife, as a reminder that I hadn't killed myself that day.

I was in the bathtub even longer on Friday, but I still didn't shoot myself. This time I wanted to. Desperately. I was biting down so hard on the barrel that when my front tooth cracked I thought for a second that the gun had fired. I'm not sure what ultimately kept me from pulling the trigger, probably cowardice, but in the end I had a second unused bullet and another date.

This became a daily ritual. Sometimes it got really, really bad. There were times, usually late at night, when literally the only thing keeping me from killing myself was the sight of the bag of bullets, the knowledge that I'd survived each of those days, so why couldn't I survive just one more?

As the sack of bullets grew heavier, it became easier not to want to pull the trigger. My life became less about escape and more about the realization that I couldn't hide away forever. I didn't need to. I'd made it through one hundred and fourteen days.

On the hundred and fifteenth day, I decided that the bullets were no longer necessary. That chilly evening I dropped the revolver in the sack, tied it tight, and walked the six miles to the Winston Bridge. As I tried to ignore the happy father walking on the other side, his daughter perched up on his shoulders, I prepared to fling the sack into the river below and begin a new era of my life.

But then I looked at the father again, burst into tears, and walked to the nearest bar, where I got so drunk that I knocked myself unconscious when I fell off the barstool. I woke up outside with blood in my eyes and the change missing from my pockets.

> I just lay on the ground, shivering, unable to see anything beyond my breath misting in the air, trying to remember if there had ever been happier times.

Not fun stuff. And this is the opening to my book, meaning that readers are immediately confronted with a suicidal narrator, which doesn't exactly promise an entertaining reading experience. Sure, the tone lightens quite a bit in the next chapter, but am I going to lose a big chunk of my readership before they even finish the prologue?

This prologue needs some humor. But of course the narrator *is* suicidal, and the tone *is* grim, and I can't lose that. So here's the actual published version, cut down a little to diminish the perception that I'm trying to pad out this article:

> I'd spent that entire morning in my bathtub, tears streaming down my face, the barrel of a revolver in my mouth, garbage bags taped to the wall so the landlord wouldn't have to repaint.
>
> There were times, usually late at night, when literally the only thing keeping me from killing myself was the sight of the bag of bullets, the knowledge that I'd survived each of those days, so why couldn't I survive just one more? Other times I'd casually put the gun to my head for half a second and then plop down on the couch and watch some TV.
>
> On the hundred and fifteenth day, I decided that in my miserable financial situation, I probably had better things to spend my money on than bullets I wasn't shooting. That chilly evening I dropped the revolver in the sack, tied it tight, and walked the six miles to the Winston Bridge. As I tried to ignore the happy father walking on the other side, his daughter perched up on his shoulders, I prepared to fling the sack into the river below and begin a new era

of my life.

Then I thought, no, bad idea. The last thing I needed was for the sack to wash up on shore and some kids to find it. I'd just have to begin the new era of my life without a symbolic act.

I looked at the father again, burst into tears, and walked to the nearest bar, where I got so drunk that I knocked myself unconscious when I fell off the barstool. I woke up outside with blood in my eyes and the change missing from my pockets. I'm sure I would have shot myself that night, except that they'd also taken the sack with my gun and bullets.

Same downbeat content, lighter tone.

Right away we've got the line "garbage bags taped to the wall so the landlord wouldn't have to repaint." Just because he wants to blow his brains out doesn't mean he has to be inconsiderate, right? This establishes the narrator's character a bit better, makes the scene more vivid, and takes a bit of the sting out of beginning the novel with a gun in the narrator's mouth.

I could've taken this a bit further:

"...garbage bags taped to the wall so the landlord wouldn't have to repaint, and a fresh can of Scrubbing Bubbles to help them clean out the bathtub afterward."

Too silly? I think so. And not particularly believable. Scrubbing Bubbles is funnier than the garbage bags, but inappropriate to both the character and the tone of the book, so I'll draw the line at the garbage bags.

"Other times I'd casually put the gun to my head for half a second and then plop down on the couch and watch some TV."

This one's a bit trickier. Admittedly, I'm going for a somewhat quirky tone with this book, and so I think it works. However, if I weren't going for that quirky tone, this might be a bit much. A possible revision could be:

"Other times I'd put the gun to my head and hold it there for a full ten seconds, to prove that I could do so without pulling the trigger, and then plop down on the couch and watch some TV."

I prefer the "half a second" version myself, but in a truly serious work of fiction the second one would be more appropriate.

The other two moments of humor, the narrator deciding that he's really too broke to keep buying bullets, and changing his mind about flinging the bullets into the water for fear that kids might find them, allow real-life concerns to intrude upon symbolic actions. How many of you watched the end of *Titanic* and thought "Don't throw that priceless necklace into the ocean! Are you friggin' CRAZY?!?" Both bits of humor are appropriate to the narrator's personality, believable, and they keep the prologue from being relentlessly depressing.

Adding comic relief to a scene of intense emotion or intense suspense is a bit more difficult. Not the humor itself, necessarily, but knowing *where* to put it. You want to give the reader a chance to gasp for breath (or dab at their eyes) without ruining the effect you've achieved. So, when you're incorporating humor into a scene like this, ask yourself these questions:

1. - Is the humor believable?

2. - Is the humor right in the middle of rising tension or emotion? (It shouldn't be. If the killer is chasing your heroine down the hallway and he's ALMOST ABOUT TO GET HER you don't want her to suddenly think, "Oh my God, I'm going to die in this ugly nightgown my mother bought me!" Instead, wait until the tension evens out, when she's hiding in the closet, desperately hoping he won't find her.)

3. - Can you shift right back to the terror/emotion/whatever? You don't want the reader to still be chuckling about the ugly nightgown two pages later when the killer has his knife to the heroine's throat.

Humor can often be used to "soften" the reader for a blow to come. Your heroine thinks she's momentarily safe...she hopes she doesn't have to die in this ugly nightgown...the reader relaxes...*then* the killer throws open the closet door!

Writing humor is a tricky beast. On one hand, it's pure instinct. You can sit there with a comedy-writing handbook and think of juxtapositions, reversals, exaggerations, and the "rule of three" all day long, but if you don't have an instinct for what's funny, it's just not gonna make people laugh. And yet on the other hand, humor writing requires more attention to word choice, rhythm, and other technical details than probably any other kind of writing apart from poetry.

So, essentially, humor writing is raw instinct mixed with bashing your head against the desk for forty-five minutes trying to think of the perfect adverb. Have fun!

CHAPTER 15

Joe R. Lansdale

Cross Reading

JOE R. LANSDALE is the multi-award winning author of thirty novels and over two hundred short stories, articles and essays. He has written screenplays, teleplays, comic book scripts, and teaches creative writing and screenplay writing occasionally at Stephen F. Austin State University. He has received The Edgar Award, The Grinzani Prize for Literature, seven Bram Stoker Awards, and many others. His stories, *Bubba Hotep* and *Incident On And Off A Mountain Road*, were both filmed. He is the founder of the martial arts system *Shen Chuan*, and has been in the International Martial Arts Hall of Fame four times. He lives in East Texas with his wife, Karen.

Reading and writing in the same genre is all right, but sometimes, if you're too familiar with the ropes and approaches to a certain type of fiction, your brain not only becomes comfortable, it becomes bored. And so does the reader.

To some extent the reader, who may read a book over a period of a day to a week, can read a book similar to the last one they read, which in the case of many, might have been months ago, and be perfectly satisfied. The writer, on the other hand, has to deal with his subject matter for months before turning the book loose into the wilds of the reading public for it to be consumed in a few hours. The writer may in fact become trapped within his- or her own success and find that as soon as they wrap up one book, they are now into writing another with familiar characters and situations.

One thing that keeps this from happening, outside of dedicated intent, and some inborn talent, is a refreshing of the brain by moving outside of your comfort zone as both reader and writer.

I grew up on science fiction and fantasy and horror, and I love all of it, and I still read in those fields, and still enjoy films in those genres, comics, etc., but I learned long ago that if all you do is write and read the same sort of books and stories you've already read, it's a little like being trapped in a stalled elevator with a freshly converted Jehovah Witness with a box of religious pamphlets. It's going to be a long and dull wait; it's going to get old, even if in the end, out of desperation, you accept salvation in exchange for silence.

When I was growing up, I had no idea that one type of reading was better for me than another, and like many bright and isolated children, I was drawn to stories of the fantastic. This was one of the best things that ever happened to me. Ignorance of what was supposed to be good, and the discovery of a form of literature that is now more widely read and respected, and has in fact, gone mainstream. This ignorance allowed me to be drawn to whatever I wanted to read, not for the purpose of enlightenment, but for the purpose of satisfaction.

I was the kind of reader that read anything available, aspirin bottle labels, directions for making malt-o-meal, whatever was in front of me. It was as if words were vitamins and I needed them to survive. Even to this day I'm an avid reader. Averaging two or three books a week, which compared to my one a day for many years, seems almost leisurely.

Even now, I have times when I'm a book glutton and will take a few days off and read one after another, resulting occasionally in a book a day or two a day if the books are short. I was blessed with the ability to read fast without skimming, and it has proven me well. So, in those early years I read a lot of books of all kinds, but primarily I read fantastic fiction of some ilk or another, (most books of this sort were less than two hundred pages back then, I might add) so when I started writing I settled on that field as my chosen vocation.

As I grew older, and spent a lot of life working hard scrabble jobs, and struggling to put bread on the table, my personal experiences became important to me as a writer, and my reading changed. Crime fiction of the hardboiled variety became more interesting to me because the characters seemed more like the people I knew. Both good and bad. Blue-collar folks with hard ways and quick wits and no rockets to the moon in sight.

I also began to discover that fiction no longer grabbed me if the characters and an engaging style were absent. It became important to me for a book to read smoothly and intelligently, and for there to be, at least in most cases, some echo beyond the reading. This is not to say that I don't like a good fun story that has nothing in its agenda but that you kill an hour or two, but it became more imperative to me, that more frequently, the story should have something about it that seemed welded to the writer who wrote it. The story needed to be a story that I felt could only have been written by that writer. Ray Bradbury is an example. He offered this kind of story. If I read something by Bradbury, it wasn't interchangeable with any other writer. Only Bradbury could write the kind of stories he wrote; he couldn't be replaced by John Doe. The beauty of the words and the capacity of the idea, the depth of the thematic content, became more important to me than forward momentum. It was no longer about wanting to read a science fiction tale, a crime story, or whatever. It was about reading a particular writer, no matter what they wrote. And what I wanted to do was become that kind of writer, the sort that when someone picks up your work, even if your name isn't on the fiction, they know who wrote it because of a certain attitude or style.

Someone like Bradbury. Like Vonnegut. Like Hemingway. You get the idea.

I wanted the reader, not to come looking for a mystery novel, a crime novel, what have you, I wanted them to come looking for a Joe Lansdale book. I wanted to have name recognition for who I was, and what I wrote. Not just be someone who filled the rack with an interchangeable story with an interchangeable style and interchangeable characters. If I was going to imitate someone, I wanted to at least be guilty of imitating myself.

So I read crime. And then I read westerns. I read more science fiction. I read horror.

Then, one morning, I awoke, glutted, satiated with all these genres, all these forms. I looked at what I was doing—and mind you, this was early in my career—and felt that all I was accomplishing was a regurgitation of what had gone before. I wanted a fresh eye. I had read a number of the classic literary writers during my college days (never got that degree) and I began to re-read them. I really got them this time, and this spun off into reading some of the offbeat literary guys like William S. Burroughs and others. I didn't love them all, but they all had something going for them that were missing in a lot of the genre novels I had read. They had what Bradbury had, what Theodore Sturgeon had, what Raymond Chandler had, what James Cain had—a point of view and a style that accomplished more than moving the plot forward, something that placed them outside the norm.

For a while, I was lost in the reading and re-reading of classic novels and stories by Hemingway, Fitzgerald, Steinbeck, Harper Lee, Mark Twain, Jack London, William Faulkner, Flannery O'Conner, William Golding, John Cheever, George Orwell, Philip Roth, William Goldman, so many others. When I was young these books had not appealed to me, with the exception of Twain and London and Harper Lee, but now I saw a maturity and control and depth of design that had mostly eluded me when I was younger and had touched on their work. Now I adored them.

And then in time, I went back to the fields that had first interested me. Books that had to do with S.F., horror and the fantastic. I had a new eye; a more literary eye. I found that writers like Shirley Jackson, Stephen King, and a handful of others, were, like Bradbury, using the furniture of horror and gothic fiction, fantasy and S.F., to not only catch the reader with the glitter and gore and bright lights of these genres, but were in fact using the fiction to get at deeper themes of alcoholism, being a parent, dealing with loneliness . . . you name it, they were doing it. Only now I got it. I was no longer drawn just to an author or one form of fiction, I was drawn to certain writers. I read plays and screenplays and comic book scripts, you name it. Anything where the writer had a real point of view, a personal vision.

Now, when I wrote, I borrowed from the writers I had read as a child, the ones who knew about catching a reader with an appealing story, and I borrowed from writers who knew how to frame a sentence, or build a character, or slip in a theme. I borrowed from those writers who had always done both. I borrowed ideas from film and comics and radio shows.

Reading not only became an even greater joy, so did writing. And in time, by learning, or at least trying to learn the tricks of the trade, I became better. My work began to blend elements from dozens of writers. I mixed in my life experience, and one day I stood up from my typewriter (this was before Word Processors were the thing), and I had written my first true Joe Lansdale story. It was mine. There was something about it, some attitude, something about the voice, the content that was mine. It wasn't a masterpiece. But it was mine. I had worn some of the clothes of other writers in previous stories, but when I looked at this story, I knew I had finally tapped into something inside of me that mattered. And I had done it by moving outside of genres, away from that sort of thinking altogether. I was writing a story that I felt only one writer could write. Me. And if it had to have a genre label on it, then I wanted to create the Lansdale genre.

Now, I admit I don't manage this all the time. But I try. And when I do manage it, it is owing to one factor and one factor only. I cross read, and I cross blend. You can't do this consciously. Mixing a Western and a Horror theme is not the same thing as actually cross blending. This comes from reading so many different kinds of works, and enjoying them, digging into your own feelings, your past, the dusty road of your experience—good or bad—and pulling it all out and throwing it in the blender and turning that baby on whip.

When you pour out the finished product, the ingredients are no longer visible. It is now what it is; A perfectly blended concoction.

Your fiction.

As Bruce Lee said, or words to the effect about martial arts: My truth may not be your truth. You should find your own truth.

You find that truth through experience. Bruce Lee felt cross training was part of the way you found that truth. The punching arts. The locking arts. The kicking arts. The throwing arts. Grappling arts. Cross training is a kind of metaphor for cross reading. Popular fiction. Literary fiction. Experimental fiction. Plays. Screenplays. Poetry. Cross reading makes you a better writer. In fact, it makes you a better reader.

Cross pollination with other types of stories can produce for anyone a better result, because even if you and I read the same books, what we get from them, the way they blend will be unique. We all bring our own vision and experience to a story, and a good story demands that we create at least fifty percent of it. We visualize the characters, the scenes, the action, the events based on our lives. We feel the emotions based on our own emotions. We bring our own uniqueness to every story we read, and we should bring that to every story we write.

After all, uniqueness is what's it's all about.

CHAPTER 16

Brian Keene

Time, and How to Make It

BRIAN KEENE is the author of over twenty books, including *Castaways, Ghost Walk, Kill Whitey, Unhappy Endings, Ghoul* and many more. He also writes for Marvel Comics. His novel *Terminal,* debuted as a stage play in 2009 and is also in development as a major motion picture. His short story, *The Ties That Bind,* was recently released as an independent film. The winner of two Bram Stoker awards, Keene's work has been featured in such places as *The New York Times,* CNN.com, The Howard Stern Show, The History Channel, *Publisher's Weekly, Fangoria Magazine,* and *Rue Morgue Magazine.* You can find him online at www.briankeene.com.

Quite often, aspiring writers will tell me all about the great novel they're working on. They'll talk of the 2,000-page outline they've written, the hours of research that have gone into it, and their plans for a full line of media tie-ins.

When I ask them how much of it is actually written, they stare at me with expressions of shock and dismay.

Don't worry. Everybody does that at the beginning.

Here's the thing. Unless you are independently wealthy, you probably have a job. Even if you don't, you probably have other responsibilities—children, a significant other, yard work, Christmas decorations to take down, a deck to stain, etc.

We lead busy lives, and with the pace of today's society, that will only increase. How then, does one get a novel or short story written in addition to everything else?

DRIVE and DEDICATION.

Books and stories do not write themselves, yet it's amazing how many people (including some very successful authors) seem to think otherwise. Writing a novel or a short story takes one thing and one thing only—sitting your rear in the chair and writing it. Posting on a message board does not help you finish. Neither does checking your email or playing a video game or looking at porn or any of the other things we do with our computers.

So let's say you've been at work all day. You come home, and you've got a free hour before dinner. You turn on the computer, go to your favorite message board, and post a thread lamenting how your novel still isn't finished because you can't find any free time to work on it. Do you see the irony here? Do you understand why you deserve to be kicked in the groin? You *have* the free time. You're just not using it.

I have been writing full time (meaning I make enough money as a writer to support my family without working a second job) for almost five years now. But before that, I worked one, sometimes two jobs. They varied; everything from foundry worker to truck driver to telemarketer to daycare instructor. Sometimes the hours were quite long. But I still made time to write each and every day. At one point in my life, I was homeless for a brief time. Even under those circumstances, I still wrote every day.

There is no such thing as finding time to write. This is a fallacy. If you look for time to write, you won't find it. Instead, you'll find something else to do.

Forget *finding* time to write. What you have to do is *make* time to write. How and when is up to you. Personally, I recommend writing every day, or at least five days a week. Writing is something that you get better at the more you do it, and therefore, it's important that you do it as often as possible.

Some very successful authors still have day jobs. Sometimes, this is by choice (they love their original profession). Other times, it's because their writing doesn't quite bring in enough income to fully support their family. But in either case, these authors still manage to continually craft and sell one or two novels per year, plus short stories, all while holding down another job and honoring their other commitments. How? They make time to write. Michael Laimo takes the train to work every day. He writes during his commute. Bev Vincent gets up extra early and writes for an hour before he goes to work. James A. Moore stays up late and writes after his family has gone to bed.

Now, each person has his- or her own individual way of working. I do my best work either very early in the morning or very late at night, and I've adjusted my schedule accordingly. But you can re-wire that if you need to. When I worked a day job, I wrote for two hours every evening. Not my optimum time for creative output, but after a few weeks my muse adapted to it.

Here is how you make time to write.

First, if you live by yourself, then we shouldn't even be having this discussion. For the sake of argument, we'll assume you have a significant other. Sit down with them and explain how important this is to you. It's not a hobby. It's not a whim. It's not some pipedream that you'll get bored with two months down the road. Make absolutely certain that they understand your dedication and drive. Trust me, it will save you many future headaches. If you're at all like me, then you're in this for the long haul, meaning you don't stop until you die. So make sure they understand that as long as you are together, this will be something that you have to do. Ask for their support. You'll need it. (And if they need advice on living with a writer, point them towards my wife's Blog, which is so funny and poignant that I'm thinking of having it shut down for libel).

Once they understand that you're serious about this, make some time for yourself. Make an hour in the day. Get up earlier. Go to bed later. Do it on your lunch break. Whatever. How and when is up to you, but MAKE IT. Be sure that your loved ones understand the importance of this hour. You are not to be disturbed. It's just like you're at work, even if you're really on a laptop and card table wedged between the hot water heater and the spare closet. No distractions. No phone calls. No, "Honey, can you open this jar of pickles." No, "Daddy, can you tell Billy to stop picking my nose." This is your time. Your hour.

And you'd better use it, because you're asking your significant other to make a sacrifice. It's only fair that you repay their support by actually producing. That means no Internet. No message boards. No researching. No checking email. None of the things that we tell ourselves constitute writing, because they don't. Writing involves one thing and one thing only—typing words on the screen.

Your average short story (based on market demand) is 3,500 words. The average person, in one hour's time, writes 500 words. If you write one hour a day, at the end of the week, you have a completed short story. The average novel (based on market demand) is 90,000 words. If you write one hour a day, at the end of the year, you have a completed novel.

It really is that simple.

So what are you waiting for?

CHAPTER 17

Deborah LeBlanc

A Face By Any Other Name

DEBORAH LEBLANC is an award-winning author and business owner from Lafayette, Louisiana. She's also a licensed death scene investigator and an active member of two national paranormal investigation teams. She is the president of the Horror Writers Association, president of the Writers' Guild of Acadiana, president of Mystery Writers of America's Southwest Chapter, and an active member of Sisters in Crime, Novelists Inc, and International Thriller Writers Inc. In 2004, she created the LeBlanc Literacy Challenge, an annual national campaign designed to encourage more people to read, and founded Literacy Inc. a non-profit organization dedicated to fighting illiteracy in America's teens. She also takes her passion for literacy and a powerful ability to motivate to high schools around the country. Her most recent novel is *Water Witch*. Visit her at www.deborahleblanc.com or www.literacyinc.com.

Occasionally I'm asked, "Do the ideas for your characters come from people you know?"

Now usually the question is asked by someone I know, so I'm figuring what they are really wanting to know is, "Am I in the book?"

In truth, the answer is, "Umm . . .well . . .yes and no." I might use your facial tick but his mustache, her eyes, and my neighbor's Aunt Betty's speech pattern to create a character. It's a lot more fun for me to take bits and pieces from people I know, have met, or have seen and create a character than it is for me to copy the exact profile of one particular person. (Hmm, I wonder if that was Dr. Frankenstein's logic...) The key to this piecemeal method is to always have a fresh supply of bits and pieces.

One supply source for me comes from people watching. No matter where I go, I'm always on the lookout for a unique face, unconscious habits, speech patterns, interactions with objects (rushed shopper gets last cart, and it has a wobbly wheel), or other people (bored husband shopping with bargain hunting wife...actually, I'd find it more interesting to watch a bored wife with bargain hunting husband!) and body language. To me, these things are the true communicators when it comes to 'knowing' a person, so the same should be considered when creating a character.

Along with people watching, I keep an eye on certain magazines and the obituaries in the newspaper, looking for unusual faces and names. If I find any, I cut them out, then sort them by category and age range... Caucasian children, Asian children, African American male, Indonesian female, Old Caucasian male, etc. The names are just sorted by male and female (first and last names separated). Now most of the time when I'm starting a story, I'll already have a main character's gender, age, and certain traits in mind, so all I have to do is go to the age group / gender file and find a face that fits. Once that's done, I'll dump out the appropriate first name file, the last name file, then piece together a name that fits the face I've just chosen.

Here's an example of how this whole process works....

People Watching: I was in a neighborhood grocery store one day, standing in line at the checkout counter, when a young African American woman comes into the store. She grabs a pack of gum, then pushes her way to the front of the line, all the while talking to herself. When she reaches the counter, she throws the gum at the register, then starts rocking in place and plucking at a button on her blouse. Everyone in line got pretty nervous and sort of backed away en masse.

Story Idea (Family Inheritance): In one scene, I have one of the main characters visiting the commons area in a mental institution. While trying to visualize what might be going on in there during her visit, I thought of the woman in the grocery store. With her in mind, I went to my African American female folder and started looking at faces. Nothing seemed to fit, even though in real life, the woman had in fact been African American. I knew the female character in this particular scene had to have a certain 'look' about her—something in her eyes that would carry to the rest of her face. I couldn't put my finger on what that something was, but I knew I'd know it when I saw it. Sure enough, I found her in the Caucasian female folder. Now I had the scene, the character traits, and the face, all I needed was a name. Out comes the female, first names folder, and within a minute or two, Terri was born. (Oh, and I also used the reaction from the people in line in that scene, too.)

Okay, I realize that all this cutting, sorting, matching sounds like a lot of work, but for me, having a clear picture of all the players helps the flow of the story.

Then again, I have to confess there are times I take the easy way out, especially with nasty, pompous, arrogant, egotistical characters. I just visualize one or two of my relatives.

CHAPTER 18

Ramsey Campbell

The Height of Fear

The *Oxford Companion to English Literature* describes RAMSEY CAMPBELL as "Britain's most respected living horror writer." He has been given more awards than any other writer in the field, including the Grand Master Award of the World Horror Convention, the Lifetime Achievement Award of the Horror Writers Association and the Living Legend Award of the International Horror Guild. Among his novels are *The Face That Must Die, Incarnate, Midnight Sun, The Count of Eleven, Silent Children, The Darkest Part of the Woods, The Overnight, Secret Story, The Grin of the Dark* and *Thieving Fear.* Forthcoming are *Creatures of the Pool* and *The Seven Days of Cain.* His collections include *Waking Nightmares, Alone with the Horrors, Ghosts and Grisly Things, Told by the Dead and Just Behind You,* and his non-fiction is collected as *Ramsey Campbell, Probably.* His novels *The Nameless* and *Pact of the Fathers* have been filmed in Spain. His regular columns appear in *All Hallows, Prism, Dead Reckonings* and *Video Watchdog.* He is the President of the British Fantasy Society and of the Society of Fantastic Films. Ramsey lives on Merseyside with his wife Jenny. His pleasures include classical music, good food and wine, and whatever's in that pipe. His web site is at www.ramseycampbell.com.

"Writers [of horror fiction], who used to strive for awe and achieve fear, now strive for fear and achieve only disgust." — David Aylward, *The Revenge of the Past*

Let's rediscover awe and supernatural dread.

I often cite the comment by the Canadian critic David Aylward I've quoted above. It strikes me as very possibly the single most important observation I've read about the field. Of course it isn't true of all horror writers, but given the growing number who seem to have no ambition beyond outdoing one another in disgustingness, it's more to the point than ever. ("It is very easy to be nauseating," M. R. James—to whom we'll return—once said.) I'd like to concentrate on elements that have made the best work in the field great and still do.

Here are the opening lines of one of the earliest classics:

> During the whole of a dull, dark, and soundless day in the autumn of the year, when the clouds hung oppressively low in the heavens, I had been passing alone, on horseback, through a singularly dreary tract of country; and at length found myself, as the shades of the evening drew on, within view of the melancholy House of Usher. I know not how it was—but, with the first glimpse of the building, a sense of insufferable gloom pervaded my spirit. I say insufferable; for the feeling was unrelieved by any of that half-pleasurable, because poetic, sentiment, with which the mind usually receives even the sternest natural images of the desolate or terrible. I looked upon the scene before me—upon the mere house, and the simple landscape features of the domain—upon the bleak walls—upon the vacant eye-like windows—upon a few rank sedges—and upon a few white trunks of decayed trees—with an utter depression of soul which I can compare to no earthly sensation more properly than to the after-dream of the reveller upon opium—the bitter lapse

> into everyday life—the hideous dropping off of the veil. There was an iciness, a sinking, a sickening of the heart—an unredeemed dreariness of thought which no goading of the imagination could torture into aught of the sublime. What was it—I paused to think—what was it that so unnerved me in the contemplation of the House of Usher? It was a mystery all insoluble; nor could I grapple with the shadowy fancies that crowded upon me as I pondered. I was forced to fall back upon the unsatisfactory conclusion, that while, beyond doubt, there are combinations of very simple natural objects which have the power of thus affecting us, still the analysis of this power lies among considerations beyond our depth. It was possible, I reflected, that a mere different arrangement of the particulars of the scene, of the details of the picture, would be sufficient to modify, or perhaps to annihilate its capacity for sorrowful impression; and, acting upon this idea, I reined my horse to the precipitous brink of a black and lurid tarn that lay in unruffled lustre by the dwelling, and gazed down—but with a shudder even more thrilling than before—upon the remodelled and inverted images of the gray sedge, and the ghastly tree-stems, and the vacant and eye-like windows.

I hope I needn't identify this as the work of Edgar Allan Poe, whose influence still lives in Stephen King. If you don't know the tale—"The Fall of the House of Usher"—you've a treat in store. Like all good writing, it gains by being read aloud. Savour the rhythm of the language, the assonance of the words, the emphatic use of alliteration and the echoing of sounds. Poe had a poet's eye and sense of language, and brought them to his prose. Like his successors Lovecraft and Ligotti, he sometimes embeds within his tales a discussion of the aesthetics of terror: see the middle of the paragraph above. Most pertinently to why we're here, the excerpt demonstrates the power of atmospheric preparation. Nothing has happened so far, and yet the awful house, which shares a soul with its doomed occupants, has been brought to undead life.

If Poe was the founder of the modern horror story in America, J. Sheridan Le Fanu deserves the British accolade. Like Poe, he concentrated the Gothic, sharpening the psychological focus, and intensified the sense of supernatural dread. In his tales the supernatural often reflects the psychology of the characters, especially elements they've tried to suppress, but can't be explained away by it (though his physician character Dr Hesselius has a stab). Like Poe, he excels at (to use Lovecraft's phrase) dread suspense. Here's the first encounter with the demonic persecutor in "Green Tea":

> "I had met with a man who had some odd old books, German editions in mediaeval Latin, and I was only too happy to be permitted access to them. This obliging person's books were in the City, a very out-of-the-way part of it. I had rather out-stayed my intended hour, and, on coming out, seeing no cab near, I was tempted to get into the omnibus which used to drive past this house. It was darker than this by the time the 'bus had reached an old house, you may have remarked, with four poplars at each side of the door, and there the last passenger but myself got out. We drove along rather faster. It was twilight now. I leaned back in my corner next the door ruminating pleasantly.
>
> "The interior of the omnibus was nearly dark. I had observed in the corner opposite to me at the other side, and at the end next the horses, two small circular reflections, as it seemed to me of a reddish light. They were about two inches apart, and about the size of those small brass buttons that yachting men used to put upon their jackets. I began to speculate, as listless men will, upon this trifle, as it seemed. From what centre did that faint but deep red light come,

and from what—glass beads, buttons, toy decorations—was it reflected? We were lumbering along gently, having nearly a mile still to go. I had not solved the puzzle, and it be came in another minute more odd, for these two luminous points, with a sudden jerk, descended nearer and nearer the floor, keeping still their relative distance and horizontal position, and then, as suddenly, they rose to the level of the seat on which I was sitting and I saw them no more.

"My curiosity was now really excited, and, before I had time to think, I saw again these two dull lamps, again together near the floor; again they disappeared, and again in their old corner I saw them. So, keeping my eyes upon them, I edged quietly up my own side, towards the end at which I still saw these tiny discs of red.

"There was very little light in the 'bus. It was nearly dark. I leaned forward to aid my endeavour to discover what these little circles really were. They shifted position a little as I did so. I began now to perceive an outline of something black, and I soon saw, with tolerable distinctness, the outline of a small black monkey, pushing its face forward in mimicry to meet mine; those were its eyes, and I now dimly saw its teeth grinning at me.

"I drew back, not knowing whether it might not meditate a spring. I fancied that one of the passengers had forgot this ugly pet, and wishing to ascertain something of its temper, though not caring to trust my fingers to it, I poked my umbrella softly towards it. It remained immovable—up to it—through it. For through it, and back and forward it passed, without the slightest resistance..."

It's the attention to detail that produces the suspense, just as Hitchcock often conveyed it by isolating details with close-up and montage. The minutely realistic observation doesn't just bring the moment alive; it lends the fantastic a foundation of realism, exactly what supernatural fiction needs. The very gradual realisation of what the character is seeing adds to the sense of unease. Horror can be all the more disturbing if it is initially misperceived.

Several of the greatest tales of supernatural terror are by Algernon Blackwood. His masterpiece, "The Willows", may be the single finest example of the horror story that reaches for awe. It's impossible to represent with an excerpt—it gains too much of its power from the accumulation of detail at novella length—and so I recommend you to read it whole. At his best Blackwood finds quite as much terror in conventional material. In "The Empty House" the protagonist and his aunt explore a house with a ghostly reputation. The idea was already familiar when the tale appeared more than a century ago, but here's a sample of how Blackwood handles it:

> Aunt Julia always declared that at this moment she was not actually watching him, but had turned her head towards the inner room, where she fancied she heard something moving; but, at any rate, both positively agreed that there came a sound of rushing feet, heavy and very swift—and the next instant the candle was out!
>
> But to Shorthouse himself had come more than this, and he has always thanked his fortunate stars that it came to him alone and not to his aunt too. For, as he rose from the stooping position of balancing the candle, and before it was actually extinguished, a face thrust itself forward so close to his own that he could almost have touched it with his lips. It was a face working with passion; a man's face, dark, with thick features, and angry, savage eyes. It belonged to a common man, and it was evil in its ordinary normal expression, no doubt, but as he saw it, alive with intense, aggressive emotion, it

> was a malignant and terrible human countenance.
>
> There was no movement of the air; nothing but the sound of rushing feet—stockinged or muffled feet; the apparition of the face; and the almost simultaneous extinguishing of the candle.
>
> In spite of himself, Shorthouse uttered a little cry, nearly losing his balance as his aunt clung to him with her whole weight in one moment of real, uncontrollable terror. She made no sound, but simply seized him bodily. Fortunately, however, she had seen nothing, but had only heard the rushing feet, for her control returned almost at once, and he was able to disentangle himself and strike a match.
>
> The shadows ran away on all sides before the glare, and his aunt stooped down and groped for the cigar case with the precious candle. Then they discovered that the candle had not been *blown* out at all; it had been *crushed* out. The wick was pressed down into the wax, which was flattened as if by some smooth, heavy instrument.

There are infelicities of style here; "ordinary normal", for instance, seems tautological. All the same, the scene is dauntingly vivid. Blackwood hasn't simply repeated a traditional motif, he has reimagined it, as all good writers do with their material. Part of the business of writing—the best way to avoid cliché—is to make us look afresh at things we may have taken for granted. What makes the apparition especially daunting, I think, is that it isn't quite where we're led to expect it to be.

So far all the excerpts have been deliberately paced, but the crucial element is the choice of language. The best tales of terror create their effects by finding the perfect word. As in comedy, timing is crucial too. The Edwardian ghost story author M. R. James was able to convey more horror in an apparently casual glancing phrase than most of us can achieve in a sentence. Sometimes he makes his nightmare creatures all the more monstrous by not describing them as such. From "The Ash-Tree", for instance:

> So the day passed quietly, and night came, and the party dispersed to their rooms, and wished Sir Richard a better night.
>
> And now we are in his bedroom, with the light out and the Squire in bed. The room is over the kitchen, and the night outside still and warm, so the window stands open.

There is very little light about the bedstead, but there is a strange movement there; it sees as if Sir Richard were moving his head rapidly to and fro with only the slightest possible sound. And now you would guess, so deceptive is the half-darkness, that he had several heads, round and brownish, which move back and forward, even as low as his chest. It is a horrible illusion. Is it nothing more? There! something drops off the bed with a soft plump, like a kitten, and is out of the window in a flash; another—four—and after that there is quiet again.

And here is an example of James's timing, with seven words that pounce on us like the monster in the tale. This is from the climax of "The Treasure of Abbot Thomas", where the narrator and his manservant have descended a well where treasure is hidden. The presence of the servant may seem to date the tale, but its power hasn't faded, believe me.

> "Well, I felt to the right, and my fingers touched something curved, that felt—yes—more or less like leather; dampish it was,

> and evidently part of a heavy, full thing. There was nothing, I must say, to alarm one. I grew bolder, and putting both hands in as well as I could, I pulled it to me, and it came. It was heavy, but moved more easily than I had expected. As I pulled it towards the entrance, my left elbow knocked over and extinguished the candle. I got the thing fairly in front of the mouth and began drawing it out. Just then Brown gave a sharp ejaculation and ran quickly up the steps with the lantern. He will tell you why in a moment. Startled as I was, I looked round after him, and saw him stand for a minute at the top and then walk away a few yards. Then I heard him call softly, "All right, sir," and went on pulling out the great bag, in complete darkness. It hung for an instant on the edge of the hole, then slipped forward on to my chest, and *put its arms round my neck.*
>
> "My dear Gregory, I am telling you the exact truth. I believe I am now acquainted with the extremity of terror and repulsion which a man can endure without losing his mind. I can only just manage to tell you now the bare outline of the experience. I was conscious of a most horrible smell of mould, and of a cold kind of face pressed against my own, and moving slowly over it, and of several—I don't know how many—legs or arms or tentacles or something clinging to my body. I screamed out, Brown says, like a beast, and fell away backward from the step on which I stood, and the creature slipped downwards, I suppose, on to that same step…"

It's worth noting how the horrors here are barely glimpsed if even seen. One principle James demonstrates is that in the tale of terror, less can frequently be better. I don't mean that horror should be described as indescribable (a tendency of which Lovecraft is too often unjustly accused); rather that it's ideal to show just enough to suggest far worse. Here's a last instance (by no means the only other I could cite) from James—an interlude in "Casting the Runes". Note the dry wit, given the rest of the paragraph, of the reticent first sentence.

> The night he passed is not one on which he looks back with any satisfaction. He was in bed and the light was out. He was wondering if the charwoman would come early enough to get him hot water next morning, when he heard the unmistakable sound of his study door opening. No step followed it on the passage floor, but the sound must mean mischief, for he knew that he had shut the door that evening after putting his papers away in his desk. It was rather shame than courage that induced him to slip out into the passage and lean over the banister in his nightgown, listening. No light was visible; no further sound came: only a gust of warm, or even hot air played for an instant round his shins. He went back and decided to lock himself into his room. There was more unpleasantness, however. Either an economical suburban company had decided that their light would not be required in the small hours, and had stopped working, or else something was wrong with the meter; the effect was in any case that the electric light was off. The obvious course was to find a match, and also to consult his watch: he might as well know how many hours of discomfort awaited him. So he put his hand into the well-known nook under the pillow: only, it did not get so far. What he touched was, according to his account, a mouth, with teeth, and with hair about it, and, he declares, not the mouth of a human being. I do not think it is any use to guess what he said or did; but he was in a spare room with the door locked and his ear to it before he was clearly conscious again. And there he spent the rest of a most miserable night, looking every moment for some fumbling at the door: but nothing came.

The sense of horror is as personal as the sense of humour, and not all the passages I've cited may work for you as they do for me. Here's an example of the naïve voice, which can convey horror precisely by appearing not to do so or by apparently being unaware that it does. It's from a girl's diary that forms the central narrative of Arthur Machen's story "The White People".

> I was thirteen, nearly fourteen, when I had a very singular adventure, so strange that the day on which it happened is always called the White Day. My mother had been dead for more than a year, and in the morning I had lessons, but they let me go out for walks in the afternoon. And this afternoon I walked a new way, and a little brook led me into a new country, but I tore my frock getting through some of the difficult places, as the way was through many bushes, and beneath the low branches of trees, and up thorny thickets on the hills, and by dark woods full of creeping thorns. And it was a long, long way. It seemed as if I was going on for ever and ever, and I had to creep by a place like a tunnel where a brook must have been, but all the water had dried up, and the floor was rocky, and the bushes had grown overhead till they met, so that it was quite dark. And I went on and on through that dark place; it was a long, long way. And I came to a hill that I never saw before. I was in a dismal thicket full of black twisted boughs that tore me as I went through them, and I cried out because I was smarting all over, and then I found that I was climbing, and I went up and up a long way, till at last the thicket stopped and I came out crying just under the top of a big bare place, where there were ugly grey stones lying all about on the grass, and here and there a little twisted, stunted tree came out from under a stone, like a snake. And I went up, right to the top, a long way. I never saw such big ugly stones before; they

came out of the earth some of them, and some looked as if they had been rolled to where they were, and they went on and on as far as I could see, a long, long way. I looked out from them and saw the country, but it was strange. It was winter time, and there were black terrible woods hanging from the hills all round; it was like seeing a large room hung with black curtains, and the shape of the trees seemed quite different from any I had ever seen before. I was afraid. Then beyond the woods there were other hills round in a great ring, but I had never seen any of them; it all looked black, and everything had a voor over it. It was all so still and silent, and the sky was heavy and grey and sad, like a wicked voorish dome in Deep Dendo. I went on into the dreadful rocks. There were hundreds and hundreds of them. Some were like horrid-grinning men; I could see their faces as if they would jump at me out of the stone, and catch hold of me, and drag me with them back into the rock, so that I should always be there. And there were other rocks that were like animals, creeping, horrible animals, putting out their tongues, and others were like words that I could not say, and others like dead people lying on the grass. I went on among them, though they frightened me, and my heart was full of wicked songs that they put into it; and I wanted to make faces and twist myself about in the way they did, and I went on and on a long way till at last I liked the rocks, and they didn't frighten me any more. I sang the songs I thought of; songs full of words that must not be spoken or written down. Then I made faces like the faces on the rocks, and I twisted myself about like the twisted ones, and I lay down flat on the ground like the dead ones, and I went up to one that was grinning, and put my arms round him and hugged him...

For what my experience is worth, that excerpt—the beginning of a much longer paragraph—fills me with the kind of dread I find in several of the films (horror films if ever I saw any) of David Lynch. I know few other tales of terror that convey so much by indirection, or suggest so much more than they show. The technique is still with us—see the stories of Thomas Ligotti and Mark Samuels, for instance—and I applaud its revival.

I hope the examples I've given are sufficiently varied and inspiring. It's time to sum up. The past offers many other fine examples: Lovecraft, for instance, devoted his entire career to trying to develop the perfect form for the weird tale. He constantly experimented with structure and narrative voice, which is why there's far more to his fiction than the mythos he created and the purple prose that's sometimes used against him, and also why his work is so difficult to represent here: "The Colour out of Space" is the single best introduction to his achievement, I think. But there are as many good techniques as there are good writers—modern ones certainly too. In *Rosemary's Baby*, for instance, Ira Levin creates a sense of mounting paranoia by his use of neutral prose—precisely because it doesn't tell us anything is wrong, we're infected with suspicions on behalf of the unaware heroine, and they prove to be all too justified. It's also remarkable as a horror novel told largely in dialogue. Nor should we forget Stephen King: take another look, for instance, at *The Shining* and consider how he prepares the hideous encounter in room 217—in particular how he paces the scene.

In a phrase, then, read the classics. In another, learn from them. At its best horror fiction can reach high places that few if any other genres can. Aim higher than you think you can attain. Experiment with technique. Discover what happens if you do without techniques and elements you think your fiction needs. Above all, tell as much of the truth as you can. I hope to hear of you.

CHAPTER 19

Michael Knost

The Aha! Moment

MICHAEL KNOST is an author, columnist, and editor of horror, dark fiction, and supernatural thrillers. He has written books in various genres, edited anthologies such as the *Legends of the Mountain State* series, *Spooky Tales from Mountain State Writers*, *Appalachian Holiday Hauntings* (with Mark Justice), and *Bullets and Brimstone* (also with Mark Justice). *To the Place I Belong* will be published in 2010, a novel based on a haunted coalmine in Southern West Virginia. To find out more, visit www.MichaelKnost.com.

Stop thinking you have the rejection letter market cornered. No author—despite popularity—has boasted immunity from these painful notes. And that's not necessarily a bad thing. After all, a rejection letter can serve the author just as much as it serves the publisher or editor. I'm not just talking about handwritten notes or suggestions from the editor; impersonal form responses can also make you a better writer.

I invited a close friend to submit something for one of the anthologies I was working on a few years ago and was excited when her story showed up in my mailbox. She is a fantastic writer, but I found myself unmoved by her tale. So, I had to send her a rejection letter; something I hated doing. She was very cordial, moving on to her next project, which was nominated for a Bram Stoker Award, I might add.

About three months later, the author sent an email, thanking me for the rejection letter, stating that after working on other projects, she'd reread the story and was mortified at what she had submitted. She was grateful that I did not publish the piece in question, as she feared it could have destroyed her budding career. Now this author was not writing from a beginning level, mind you, she admitted working under a number of deadlines and rushed the story in question. Something I wager she'll never do again.

However, beginning writers will obviously produce vastly inferior works in comparison with those he or she produces after years of honing the craft. Just as the hideous ashtray a world-renowned sculptor might have produced as a child is far inferior to the works of art he or she now has displayed in prestigious galleries and museums. We mature and develop as we identify our mistakes, making the most of them. That's why rejection letters, although painful, are very important.

In his book *On Writing,* Stephen King offers a rare glimpse behind the Wizard of Odd's curtain, revealing the painful scars of a young man with aspirations of a publishing career:

> "By the time I was fourteen . . . the nail in my wall would no longer support the weight of the rejection slips impaled upon it. I replaced the nail with a spike and kept on writing."

In a recent interview, Ray Bradbury spoke about his early struggles for a successful writing career:

> "It was a long, slow process with a thousand rejections. I'm still getting rejected this late in time. The important thing is to continue writing and continue being in love with books, authors, and libraries."

It's hard to fathom Ray Bradbury struggling with rejection letters, isn't it? But, if he's still receiving these tortuous slips, what makes you and

I think we deserve better? And what can we learn from this?

Keep writing. Even if you have wallpapered your writing room with rejection letters, keep writing. That's certainly good advice, but perseverance will only prolong the agony unless you *improve* your craft. So, how does one do that? Well, you have to be able to distinguish good writing from the bad.

My wife worked as a bank teller a number of years ago and related the process used for identifying counterfeit currency. "You can't spot a fake unless you can identify the genuine article," she'd said. "We study real money, immersing ourselves in it to the point that anything counterfeit sticks out like a sore thumb."

That's why we as authors should read as much of the good stuff as possible. If we study the good stories, immersing ourselves in them, we'll be able to identify the bad aspects of writing and avoid them. And every now and then, we will make a discovery that changes how we think and write forever after.

Some call it intuitive perception, some call it an epiphany, and some call it self-enlightenment. I call it the *Aha! Moment*.

You know what I'm talking about; it's that crucial moment where the light bulb comes on over your head, leading to a verbal confirmation such as, "Aha!"

Most of us have experienced many of these moments in our writing, but there is always one or two that stick out as the turning point in our career.

I asked ten writers who are just breaking into the publishing markets what their Aha! Moments were in hopes that we could gain some insight on what made their work move from rejection to acceptance. The responses are as diverse as the writing styles these talented individuals employ. I'm hoping these answers lead you to your own epiphany moments, and to less rejection letters.

Nate Kenyon found his Aha! Moment in self-editing:

> "I'd sent the first few chapters of *Bloodstone* off to Five Star and I got an email asking to see the rest. I knew from previous editors' feedback that *Bloodstone* was too long and had too many characters for a first novel. I'd tried to edit it before, but I'd been unable, or unwilling, to cut it down enough to make it work, and I'd always received the same reasons for rejection.
>
> "This time I decided to ruthlessly chop away as if I were editing someone else's manuscript rather than my own. I even made up a fake author's name to put on the cover page: *Tyson Soule*. I worked all night and by the next morning I'd cut over forty thousand words. I sliced whole characters out and streamlined the entire plot. I sent the revised novel in, and had a contract offer a short time later.
>
> "I've been much better since at taking off my *writer's* cap when the first draft is done, and putting on the *editor's* cap to make the tough decisions. For his part, Tyson isn't talking. I just hope he doesn't take it personally."

Sarah Langan's Aha! Moment came about five years into attempting to sell a few short fiction pieces and her first novel. She related her work as being a square peg that didn't fit into the conventional round holes of literary magazines like *Glimmer Train*, the now defunct *Story*, and *Zoetrope*:

> "I realized that so long as I wrote about ghosts and dead people, no matter how literate, big publishing would not accept me.
>
> "In the late 90s, genre was verboten. Single girl, Candace Bushnell crap was all over the bestseller lists, and the literary world

was obsessed with loading their first author picks with recipes. Weird but true. So I expanded my search, and for the first time since I was a teen, started reading horror and science fiction.

"I subscribed to *Cemetery Dance*, poured over Datlow's *Fantasy and Science Fiction*, and went online, and found the HWA, too. I spent another year or so learning from what I read, and figuring out what my fiction needed to work as genre, then submitted a few stories to *Chizine*. Trish Macomber, who was the fiction editor there at the time, accepted a story called Taut Red Ribbon. It was the first story I'd written without an internal sensor, and on that day, I think I found my true voice. Things got a lot easier after that, not because the doors of publishing opened or anything, but because after that, I always wrote exactly what I wanted, instead of the literary crap that bored me to tears."

John R. Little experienced his Aha! Moment while attending the inaugural Borderlands Bootcamp:

"Tom Monteleone was critiquing a story of mine and he said something to the effect that I was great at coming up with wonderful concepts and ideas, but I always forgot to include a *story*. Great concepts and interesting characters were fine, but I didn't take the time to be sure there was a rocketing plot in it. From that point, I always made sure the *story* was never lost, and my sales started taking off immediately."

Bev Vincent suffered the exact opposite. He didn't have a plot or story problem, he says his earliest works of fiction were built around plot ideas and populated by characters that served it:

"My characters didn't have much personality, and their motives were never explored or particularly obvious to anyone, including me.

"In 2000, I wrote a story about a man suffering from an OCD disorder that made him constantly sure he'd just hit someone with his car. This is a plot idea, but what elevated the story, in my opinion, was that it wasn't really about his perilous drive to a convenience store on Halloween night, when the streets were alive with potential hit-and-run victims. The story got inside his head and showed readers what it was like to be him. What were his challenges and trials and tribulations? What did he want? In a way, it inverted my approach—the plot became of service to the character, instead of the other way around.

"Harming Obsession resonated with readers, more than anything else I'd written to that point. I realized that I had to stop treating my characters like pawns on a chessboard. I used to begin new stories as soon as I had an idea. Now I wait until I have an idea and a sense of who the major players are and what motivates them. I described this revelation in an essay, saying: 'Story is what characters do when presented with a situation.' It shifted my focus away from events and onto the characters."

Mary SanGiovanni found her Aha! Moment during her studies at Seton Hill University's Master's of Popular Fiction program:

"I had read a story I wrote for the workshop, which was comprised of romance writers, SF writers, and YA writers. I had anticipated, I admit with some degree of shame, harsh critiques because of the genre writers in the group; I didn't expect them to understand horror, or what I was going for, or any of the supernatural elements and their place in the story. But when I was done reading a beginning portion of the story, we began to discuss it.

"The romance folks gave opinions and insight into the effectiveness of the character's interpersonal relationships, and the young adult folks offered suggestions on clarity for the supernatural elements. It affected one critiquer enough to make her cry, and she had to leave the room. There was a long, deep silence after that, in which one of the romance writers said (and I'm paraphrasing here), 'Well, at least you know you wrote something that touched someone.'

"That was the moment, I think, that I realized several things. One, I realized that you can learn about writing in your genre by reading and listening and understanding the strengths of writing outside your genre. A great story is a great story, regardless of genre, and the best work utilizes the skill sets and strengths of many genres.

"I also learned that, particularly in horror, which is a genre whose very foundation is pure emotion, gore for gore's sake, say, or an awesome, scary monster, or cool and creepy vignettes are all meaningless if, as a writer, you don't reach that core part of a reader where the emotions lay.

"What makes horror memorable, marketable, and enjoyable over multiple readings is the reader-to-character recognition of and relation to basic emotions. I have miles to go before succeeding on a level I'd like, but I think that learning those things changed my writing—not just in quality or marketability, but in the overall enjoyment of writing it."

Mark Justice says his Aha! Moment came while voicing an audio version of one of his stories:

"I don't know about other writers, but I have an enormous blind spot when it comes to typos. I would pour over my manuscripts, dutifully fixing all mistakes. Later, when one of my first readers would check the manuscript, another dozen or more typos would rear their ugly heads.

"My brain, it seems, sees what it wants to see, glossing over the missing or transposed letters and substituting the right word at the right spot.

"It wasn't until I was invited to produce an audio version of one of my stories for a website that I made a breakthrough. This was a story that had gone through several revisions, one that I had read at least 10 times or more. It was, I thought, as good as I could make it.

"And when I read it out loud I was mortified. I found new typos, clumsy phrasing and questionable grammar. I did a rewrite on the spot, ending up with a better story.

"Now I read everything out loud before I submit. It's made a difference in the quality of my work and in the number of acceptances.

The embarrassing part is that a guy who has worked in radio for over 30 years should have figured this out quicker."

Maurice Brauddus had a few Aha! Moment's hit him at the same time:

"I've been blessed to have a good set of mentors at every step of my career. My first one, Wayne Allen Sallee, always believed that when you were ready, a mentor would show up. He was the one who introduced me to the convention scene (literally: he convinced me to attend the World Horror Convention in 2002 and introduced me around). So lesson one came with learning to build the business side of writing by developing contacts and meeting my peers (who would become invaluable over the years).

"The second came from a workshop I attended at that same con, taught by Uncle Mort (Mort Castle). I'm a pretty good natural storyteller, but that's a far cry from (or at least only the first step in) being a good storywriter. So we were doing a writing exercise with him where he had us tell either a funny or sad story from our childhood. I wrote how I always wrote and turned in five pages. He looked it over and said, 'you realize your story doesn't begin until page three.' In one simple sentence, he diagnosed the major stumbling block to my storytelling. I needed to start the story where the story begins.

"The next year I won the short story contest at the World Horror Convention."

Nate Southard is another author that found his Aha! Moment while attending the Borderlands Boot Camp:

"I learned so much during that weekend, and it really made my writing stronger and cleaner. If I had to pick a bit of advice as the best, I'd say it was the instructors' suggestion to submit my work to top markets and trickle down, rather than try to work my way up from the bottom. I've found that communicating with these markets has done more for my career and recognition level than just about anything else I've done, and the feedback I've received from the editors of these markets has helped my writing improve by leaps and bounds. In the past few years I've seen plenty of talented writers slog through because of some outdated notion of starting at the bottom and clawing your way up. It really doesn't need to be that way."

Bob Freeman found his Aha! Moment the first time he typed the words The End after completing his novel *Shadows Over Somerset*:

> "Here's how I see it... How many times have we been at a dinner party or the local watering hole and you're chatting someone up and the question gets asked, 'So, what do you do?' Invariably, as soon as you say *writer*, your conversational foil will respond with, 'You know, I've always thought about writing a book.' How often do you think biochemists or brain surgeons hear that? The short answer is none, and it's because most people think writing is easy, until that is, they sit down to actually do the work.
>
> "I fell into that category, thinking of myself as a writer long before I had actually paid my dues, staring down the demon that is the blank page, and seeing the battle through to the bitter end. Oh, I'd started dozens upon dozens of novels, none of them getting past the first paragraph or so. Writing *is* hard work. You spill your guts with every keystroke and the ink as it strikes the paper is drawn from your own sweat and blood. Did I just show my age? I think you catch my meaning just the same.
>
> "So, yes, my first and most important battle in my quest toward becoming an author was, in my opinion, the most crucial for each and every one of us who have chosen this path. I sat myself down in a chair and I wrote the thing. And you know what, I've never looked back. Each successive novel has come easier. Of course new challenges arise, but that's okay... such is the nature of the beast."

Brian J. Hatcher's Aha! Moment came while working with a deadline:

"Framed and hanging on the wall of my home office, I have a dollar bill commemorating my first professional sale and a letter from Governor Joe Manchin III of West Virginia complimenting me on a story I'd written. Both these mementos on my wall I have because of The Hungry Earth, a short story published in the anthology *Legends of the Mountain State*. This was the story that almost didn't happen.

"Two weeks before the anthology's deadline, I realized I was in trouble. Editing wasn't going well; the problems with the story were plentiful and egregious. The characters didn't ring true, the middle collapsed like a sand castle against the coming tide, and the ending was trite and unrewarding. I came to the painful realization that the story might not be salvageable. I had another story idea, but I wasn't sure if two weeks would be enough time to get it into shape; but either I had to try or give up entirely.

"The next two weeks became my Writer's Hell. I wrote, edited, wrote more, went back to the first story to see if maybe I could somehow come up with a way to fix it, found it to be as bad as I remembered, then wrote still more. With only one day left before the deadline, I had the new story completed.

"However, I wasn't satisfied with it.

"It seemed rushed, and of course it was. I felt I needed more time, but there was none left. I considered sending Michael Knost—the editor of the anthology—an e-mail telling him I wouldn't be able to send him a story. I wanted to give up, and I almost did. Finally, I decided to send the story and hope for the best. It still took me ten minutes to assemble the courage to click the *send* button on the e-mail.

"Michael accepted the story, and the boost it gave my career and the praise I garnered for it is, as the saying goes, is history.

"It would seem the moral of this story is that I published because I finally overcame my insecurity and hypercritical nature. But that isn't true. If I would have had the confidence and courage, I'd have sent the first story; and instead of framed mementos on a wall, I would have another rejection letter, well earned.

"When I began my writing career, I had big dreams of *making it*. Writing would be easy, publishing even easier, and laurels would be gratuitously heaped upon me. The Hungry Earth helped me put away such foolish, meaningless dreams. Writing will never be easy; and for that, I am grateful. Every story I write is harder than the last. Every sentence, every word, takes an ever-growing effort. I struggle, even with these few words I write now. I get frustrated, I even consider quitting, yet I keep writing. I believe this utter inability to be satisfied is the *flamma magna*, the alchemical flame that transforms art into something greater than the artist. The fire will guide me and help me grow, as long as I don't let it burn me down. I learn more, I see more, and I want so much more from my work. Let others dream of *making it*. May I never be fulfilled. May I never look upon my work and say, 'I am content.' I would rather go to my page and say, 'Let's see if I can do better.'"

Michael West found his Aha! Moment after finding first readers outside the genre:

"I had experienced great success in the 'for the love' markets—magazines that paid very little or nothing but contributors copies, and I just could not understand why the professional (and even semi-professional) markets kept passing on my work. Then, I made the decision to open up my circle of readers. Up to this point, I'd only shone my work to people who read or watched nothing but horror. These readers were true fans of the genre, and they knew its various conventions. They were forgiving of certain aspects of my plots and characterizations, because this was the way people in a horror story act, and these were things people in horror stories do.

"However, when I started to show my fiction to readers who, in some cases, did not even *like* horror, these 'outsiders' did not look the other way on these issues. They helped me make my characters more believable, their motivations much clearer, and they allowed me to finally find my true voice. When I began to write tales about real people, with real problems, who just happened to find themselves in terrifying, unbelievable situations...I began to sell."

As a maturing writer, you should always be on the lookout for Aha! Moments. They come unexpectedly, and they almost always make such an impact that you'll see results almost immediately.

So, don't let the rejection letters discourage you. Keep writing, and pay attention to the things that will improve your craft. Your turning point could be one Aha! Moment away.

CHAPTER 20

Jason Sizemore

Be a Conformist: A Guide to Manuscript Formatting

A young Appalachian writer and editor from Kentucky, JASON SIZEMORE has seen his fiction appear in over two-dozen books and magazines. He's a prolific non-fiction writer, having dozens of essays, reviews, and editorials published in print and on the web on varied subjects such as gaming, geek culture, and politics. In 2005, Jason launched *Apex Publications* and in 2006 he was a Stoker Award nominee for his work on the anthology *Aegri Somnia.*

Too many writers have their stories dumped in the recycle bin over the simplest of things: manuscript formatting. Approximately 10-20% of submissions to *Apex Magazine* are bounced back to the authors with a rejection notice and a polite note from the editor about the need to conform to our formatting guidelines. When this happens, the writer has not only failed even to get a foot in the door, but also likely annoyed an editor.

The solution to this problem is simple: be a conformist. Fall in line with everybody else. Don't stand out. Be boring.

Perhaps that's too straightforward. Allow me to call on the wisdom of a college drinking buddy I knew many years ago named Chester Hardesty (name changed to protect the not-so-innocent). I'd reached legal drinking age, thus automatically invoking a "Rite of Passage" party thrown by my friends and classmates. And what a grand party it was. I was taught the mantra "Beer before liquor, never been sicker!" and its corollary, "Liquor before beer, in the clear!" There were frat boys circling kegs of beer like thirsty hyenas around a desert lake. A group of sorority sisters took turns charring my desk by lighting up shots of Everclear and then dropping them into glasses of Dr. Pepper. I had no idea who half these people were, but the booze was free and flowing, and people were toasting me in my honor. Good times.

Sometime during the night, ol' Chester draped his arm around my shoulders. He moved close to my face, inches away, and looked at me square in the eyes. His breath was a foul mix of Cool Ranch Doritos and Bud Light. The shot of Jagermeister I'd just downed gurgled in my stomach; I was not liking the situation.

"Don't go ticking off those guys," Chester said.

"What guys?" I asked.

"Those by the doors, you know?"

I looked around. We were in my dorm room, and three guys from my Computer Science 101 class stood nervously by the doorway. They nursed beers and watched wide-eyed in wonder.

"No way. Those guys are harmless."

This earned me a slap across the back of my head. "I'm talkin' about those big apes who stand outside the club doors…the ones that won't let you in to dance and co-mingle with the ladies."

"Co-mingle?"

"Right."

I had no idea what the man was talking about.

"Be nice and follow their rules no matter what, or you'll never get inside."

Chester then proceeded to grab me in a headlock and kiss the top of my head.

Chester's sage advice didn't make any sense to me, especially while

I was stuck underneath his sweaty armpit. But years later, when I opened *Apex Magazine* and discovered the "delights" of the slush pile, his true meaning dawned on me.

Don't tick off the editors; they are the bouncers of the writing world. This means avoiding the quickest way to annoy an editor: not following manuscript guidelines.

The problem with proper manuscript formatting is that it's one of those things that won't directly get you published, but it is something that will prevent you from getting read, and if you aren't read, you won't be published. When editors see an improperly formatted submission, a little red devil (complete with horns that look like semi-colons) appears on their shoulders and says one of the following:

"Why should I take the time to read this if the writer didn't take the time to format it the way I prefer? I have needs, too."

"What an amateur! His story probably sucks."

"Wonder why she didn't check the guidelines. She probably doesn't read the instructions on medicine bottles either, and one day it'll be her death. Snort."

There's a reason for the formatting rules, and it has nothing to do with causing poor, hassled writers more troubles. Editors are busy people, so a manuscript has to be especially good for an editor to waste time on re-formatting. Besides, editors have better ways of driving writers crazy.

Here are some basic rules of formatting you should follow (unless you're submitting to a publication that states otherwise in its guidelines):

1. - Double line spacing is the rule. A common mistake made by new writers is to single space paragraphs and double space between paragraphs. This is a common format seen in articles of text on the Internet, but it's not how editors generally want a manuscript formatted. Psychologically, when reading double spacing, the editor

feels as though he or she is whizzing through the lines. It looks cleaner and neater on the page. It allows for editorial comments and typographical markings between the lines. With modern-day word processors, none of this is difficult for the writer to achieve.

2. - Use a common and practical monospaced font. Most of the time, Courier New will suffice. A few editors I know prefer Times New Roman, so this is a case of in which doing a little bit of research might pay off.

3. - Use a readable font point size. Don't go any lower than 12 point. Don't go higher than 14 point.

4. - Leave at least an inch of white space margin on all four sides of your manuscript. This will give the editor room to make notes and will help make your submission look cleaner. The left margin of text should be justified and the right margin of text should be jagged.

5. - Use black ink on white paper and use only one side of each sheet of paper.

6. - You don't need a dedicated title page for short stories. You do for novels and novel-length collections. On the first page of your manuscript, using the upper half of the page to place your contact information and word count, followed by the story's title along with your byline.

7. - On all pages but the first, include a right justified running header with your byline, the story's title, and the page number. This is in case the editor jumbles up your pages and needs to reorder them. I

won't lie, editors are notoriously disorganized individuals. At least I am!

Master and conform to these seven basic instructions and you'll be on the path to publication.

There are many other "picky" rules of manuscript formatting. Thankfully, a gentleman named William Shunn wrote an essay that covers such quandaries as "Do I list professional organizations of which I'm a member with my contact information?" and "Do I use the Microsoft Word word count or do I have to manually count the words or use some other formula?" You can find this excellent essay (titled "Proper Manuscript Format") at www.shunn.net/format.

One trap many writers fall into is reading a publication's guidelines once and never checking again for updates. Sometimes word count ranges change, or a publication has a change in editors and now prefers Times New Roman or Courier font. Because of this, be careful when using resources such as Duotrope.com, Ralan.com, and the *Writer's Digest Guide to Short Fiction Markets*. They're useful as a first port of call, but always refer back to the official guidelines of your chosen market before sending off your baby.

As I mentioned earlier, it might pay to research a market's editorial style. This goes beyond just reading the guidelines. Do they prefer the American style of punctuation or the British style? Will they laugh at you if you put a copyright statement on the title page? Do they prefer a single space or a double space after ending punctuation? I once suffered public ridicule in a writing workshop run by a well-known science fiction editor over double spacing after punctuation. I'm still scarred by the experience. Read previous publications by that market. Read the editors' blogs. There is plenty of information out there.

When in doubt, ask. Most of the time, editors are nowhere as intimidating as those burly dudes at the club doorways. In fact, *Apex* editors like receiving questions. It makes us feel like we have friends. It makes us feel like we are important.

Follow my advice about manuscript formatting if you want to be a successful writer. *Please don't let a simple thing you can control be the one thing that gets you rejected.*

CHAPTER 21

Lisa Morton

CUT! Or, Why Writing Horror Screenplays is REALLY Scary

LISA MORTON'S most recent horror screenplay was 2004's *Blood Angels,* although she's done some uncredited (and happily so) rewrites on other films since. She is also a prolific author of non-fiction books and short horror fiction; her most recent book, 2008's *A Hallowe'en Anthology: Literary and Historical Writings Over the Centuries,* was nominated for the Black Quill Award, and in 2006 she won the Bram Stoker Award for Short Fiction. She lives in North Hollywood and can be found online at www.lisamorton.com.

So you want to write a horror movie.

Maybe you've been approached by a producer who sees cinematic potential in that last short story you published. Or maybe you just walked out of the latest ghost-slasher-torture porn-Asian remake and thought, *I could do better than that.* You've got the talent, you've got the drive, you've got the idea, and you've got this fantasy phone call in your head: "Hi, I'm a big-budget producer and I read your script, I think you're a genius, and I'm offering you seven figures right now so I can make you an overnight success, and then you and I can work together to change the entire course of horror movie history!"

That's the fantasy. The reality—if you've worked really hard and are phenomenally lucky—is likelier to be a call that goes something like this:

"Yeah, we've got this monster movie pre-sold to certain foreign territories, so I need you to write something to match the title and the poster art and I need it in two weeks. Oh, and we can't pay you Guild minimum. You're cool with that, right?"

Welcome to Hollywood.

If you're determined to stick to the fantasy, then you should probably skip the rest of this article. Good luck, and enjoy your lucrative career...as a plumber.

If, however, you're willing to listen and start from the bottom and work hard and persevere no matter what, then keep reading.

First off, let's assume you're interested in seriously pursuing a career as a screenwriter, not just toying with the format or writing a script once for your brother in Podunk because he's got a new credit card with an insanely high limit and wants to make a zombie flick. This article also isn't about how to sell rights to your novel or make your own short movie, either of which can be happy one-time events. No, this is about you focusing on becoming a honest-to-goodness working horror screenwriter, making sales and seeing your name in those opening credits.

That's what you want? Great. Then let's get right down to business, and start with a list. Here are the Top Five Things You Will Need to Make It as a Screenwriter:

1) *Live in Los Angeles*. Really. That's why it's in the number one position, above those little things like writing a great script. In publishing, you can live in Nebraska and have an agent and editor in New York you've never met, but it doesn't work that way in the film business. You'll need to start off meeting people; this isn't something you can fly in and do in a weekend (or a month, or even six months). Eventually you'll need to be here to take meetings (you might be amazed at how many movie deals are the result of meetings, not full

scripts), first with agents, then with producers and development executives.

2) *Know how to sell yourself.* Are you someone hugs the wall at parties so tightly you leave an impression...on the wall, that is? Then you should seriously consider staying at home and writing scary books. Hollywood's about the hustle; if you're not good at it, your only other option is to partner yourself with someone who is. You need to be able to present yourself well in meetings—be personable, be attractive, be fun.

3) *Get a day job.* While you're living in Los Angeles (and remember, it ain't cheap in SoCal), you'll need to support yourself. You might be tempted to go after some entry level job in the film industry—say, a production assistant—to get your foot in the door, but be warned: A.) the job will have insanely long hours and probably leave you too exhausted to write; B.) you'll run the risk of being thought of *only* as someone who is capable in that job, not as a writer; and C.) the job likely won't last beyond the current film, and then all your time will have to go into hunting down the next job again. If you're still determined to start in the film industry, consider trying to get an opening position as a script analyst (someone who reads scripts and synopsizes them for producers and companies)—the hours will be more reasonable, the work is steady, and you'll be dealing with agents and producers on a daily basis, building your contacts. However, a non-film job can work, too, and will probably offer you more time and energy to write.

4) *Software.* I know this might seem mundane, but it's a major requirement. The industry standard is Final Draft, and it's not incred-

ibly cheap; even a used copy will probably run you a few hundred bucks. There are other programs that can export in Final Draft format (I actually use Movie Magic Screenwriter myself), and the good news is that all of the major screenwriting programs are user-friendly and easy to learn.

5) *A great script*. Here's where those little things like "talent" and "knowing your genre" come into play. You're going to need a calling card as a new writer trying to break in; for an actor it's a head shot (that's a photo portrait, not a gore effect), and for a writer it's a completed script. And let's talk a little first about what I mean when I use the word "great". Do you know the genre well enough to know whether your idea has already been done to death? Can you summarize your idea in no more than two medium-length sentences? Of course there are plenty of other factors that go into making a script "great" (can you write realistic dialogue that actors can actually say, for example), but those two factors mentioned above may be what agents and producers will look at first when reading your script.

Now, let's talk a little bit more about that #5 above. Specifically, let's talk about writing a great *horror* script.

You might be tempted to ask, "Why do I need a great script? All the horror movies I've seen lately have all looked like one another. Oh, and, uh...they all sucked." While that may (or may not) be true, you need to remember a couple of things: First, no first-time writer has ever been hired on the basis of a *bad* script; and secondly, movies are a collaborative effort, and as such it's entirely possible that the crappy movie you regretted paying ten bucks to see last weekend started out as a *great* script.

Believe me, it happens. To all of us.

So, we're agreed that your script needs to be special. But here's the thing: It can't be *too* special. Want to know why nobody's made, say, a movie about a squad of cheerleaders who discover they're all incarnations of ancient Assyrian demons? Well, probably because it's a hard idea to market—what do ancient Assyrian demons look like? What can they do? How did they become cheerleaders? Movies are first and foremost commodities, and as such they need to be easy to sell to viewers; you don't want a concept that's likely to leave a potential audience member (or development executive) going, "Wha-huh?" Change the Assyrian demons to vampires, though, and now you might have a script that's far more saleable.

So you've got your idea—a group of cheerleaders who are actually vampires—and you're ready to write. You've seen every vampire movie ever made, you know the rules, you love the fangs. You've read lots of scripts and studied them, so you understand the basics (EXT. vs. INT., when to use a fade instead of a dissolve, how parentheticals work in dialogue, etc.). You know that you can figure a minute a page, and that your finished script should be as close to 100 pages as possible. Maybe you've even read something like Robert McKee's *Story* or Christopher Vogler's *The Writer's Journey* and studied three-act structure and mythic archetypes.

So how do you scare the crap out of people with a script?

First you need to decide just what kind of horror movie you're aiming for. Do you want to make those cheerleaders a little funny as well as scary? Are you thinking of something for a feature film, or for the SciFi Channel's Saturday night feature? PG or R? A good script maintains a consistent tone throughout; it doesn't start, for example, with a trickle of blood and finish with gallons spilling from dozens of severed limbs.

And speaking of which—you as the screenwriter also need some understanding of how movie budgets work. You should have a basic knowledge of art direction, stunts, special effects, sound and cinematography. Maybe you think it's incredibly cool to have those cheerleaders suddenly transform into dozens of bats with twenty-foot wingspans that swoop down inside a school amphitheater and disembowel hundreds, but I can almost guarantee you that scene will get your script thrown out instantly—it involves makeup effects, CGI, too many extras and location shooting, and is just too expensive. Scale it down to two vamp chicks who sprout fangs and seduce a pair of quarterbacks, and you're back in the game.

You also need to give your story tension. This is a horror movie, after all, and your first and foremost job is to leave that audience crushing their popcorn cups in dread. Having your head cheerleader just sink her teeth into a willing hunk's neck might be sexy, but it's not suspenseful. Have her stalk him first through a dark high school and then corner him in a classroom as he tries unsuccessfully to defend himself...and *then* let her sink her teeth into his neck. Now you've got scary *and* sexy, and that's a combination you just can't beat.

So your script is finished. You've rewritten it five times, and you think it's ready. So here comes a big question: Do you need an agent now?

Yes...and no.

If you want to work towards getting into the studios and the Writer's Guild (WGA), then yes—you absolutely need an agent. You can start by querying agents listed with the WGA (on their website at www.wga.org), but that's a long shot. You need to get out and meet people. Go to parties. Go to screenings. Go to conferences. Talk to other writers. If you've gotten to know any agents (and good for you!), ask them to read your script.

The alternative is to forge ahead into the wild and woolly world of non-union movies. Frankly, if you want to write horror movies, there are probably more of 'em being made for direct-to-DVD release and cable by these non-Guild-signatory companies, and you might even be able to get a script read by some of them without an agent, but even then you'll need an attorney or an agent to go over your contracts and negotiate on your behalf (of course if you already have a deal in hand, then scoring an agent or attorney should be easier).

Now here's where it gets really ugly: You won't be getting rich. Most of these non-union companies don't pay "Guild minimum"; in fact, you probably won't make enough off a single script sale to buy a new car, especially not after your agent takes a cut and you put some away for taxes. Don't expect to make a living going this route; you also won't get benefits like health care, pension or residuals.

Something else you need to realize: That great script about the vampire cheerleaders, the one you slaved over for months? Well, you may never sell it or see it made. Don't expect it to ever be anything more than a writing sample (or a "spec" in industry lingo). Remember that opening conversation with the producer about the pre-sold monster movie? That call might come after he's read your script and realized you have the chops—and that he can hire you cheap because you're hungry.

But hey, if you do a good job, he might hire you again for the giant spider movie. And then for the Korean ghost remake. And before long, you might be one of the lucky few who turns horror screenwriting into a career.

Just don't give up your day job too soon.

CHAPTER 22

Gary Frank

It's All About the Series: An Interview with F. Paul Wilson

GARY FRANK is the author of *Forever Will You Suffer, Institutional Memory,* and the co-editor of *Dark Territories,* the anthology from the Garden State Horror Writers. He is also the author of a number of short stories, including *Stay Here,* which was published in the 2005 anthology, *Dark Notes From New Jersey.* A member of the Horror Writers Association since 2005, Gary has also been a member of the Garden State Horror Writers since 2003, where he is just finished his two-year run as president. When he's not spilling his imagination on the page or working the day job, he's playing guitar. He's currently at work on his third novel, but that's another story.

F. PAUL WILSON is the bestselling author of more than thirty books: six science fiction novels *(Healer, Wheels Within Wheels, An Enemy Of The State, Dydeetown World, The Tery, Sims),* nine horror thrillers *(The Keep, The Tomb, The Touch, Reborn, Reprisal, Nightworld, Black Wind, Sibs, Midnight Mass),* three contemporary thrillers *(The Select, Implant, Deep As The Marrow)* and a number of collaborations. In 1998 he resurrected his popular antihero, Repairman Jack, and has chronicled his adventures in *Legacies, Conspiracies, All The Rage, Hosts, The Haunted Air, Gateways, Crisscross,* and *Harbingers.*

Gary Frank: *I'm talking with F. Paul Wilson on writing a series character. First, though, I thought I'd start with a couple of basic questions for those unfamiliar with him or his work. How long have you been writing and how'd you stumble into the horror genre?*

F. Paul Wilson: I've always been a horror fan and I wrote my first story in second grade. Well, half a story; I didn't finish it. I think you're wired for certain kinds of fiction and what appeals to you, and that's what appeals to me. I started off writing science fiction because there was no horror market. In fact, I was criticized in the 70's for my science fiction being a little too horrific. I kept sneaking it in. When King opened up the market, I decided I'd jump in and I wrote *The Keep*.

GF: *So that was your first novel?*

FPW: No, I had three science fiction novels. *Healer, Wheels Within Wheels,* and *An Enemy of the State* back in the 70's. That's when I became known as "that libertarian science fiction writer" because they were very libertarian in their outlook.

GF: *What was the first Repairman Jack novel?*

FPW: *The Tomb* and it wasn't supposed to be a series.

GF: *Weren't there three books that started things off? The Keep, The Tomb, and The Touch.*

FPW: That was The Adversary Cycle, which I didn't know was a cycle then. I just thought of *The Tomb* as the next book after *The Keep*. *The Touch* was after that, but it wasn't related to either in any way that I intended, at least consciously. Later on, I found ways to connect them that seemed to have been subconscious all along. But I did not want to do a series, which is why I left Jack dying at the end of *The Tomb*.

GF: *So what happened?*

FPW: It never went out of print and so it accrued more and more fans; people wrote letters asking to bring Jack back and I kept saying no. I saw a series as a trap and I had these other things already in my head I wanted to write. I did write Jack short stories and a novelette at the request of people like Ed Gorman and Phyllis Weinberg in various little venues and anthologies. But I told myself it wasn't a series, just a story here and there. Then the medical thrillers came in the 90's. I had a contract for three and I wrote two of them, *Implant* and *Deep as the Marrow*, and they were getting further and further away from medical thrillers because I didn't find medical thrillers all that interesting to write. I still liked to read them when they were well done, but they didn't appeal to me to write. Then I had this idea for a sort of techie thriller and the perfect protagonist would've been Jack. But book number three was supposed to be a medical thriller. So I wrote it anyway with Jack as the hero and I had him hired by a doctor. I said that makes it a medical thriller and the publisher liked the book so they ignored that little failing. That was *Legacies* and it went over very well and I had fun playing with Jack, so I said I'm going to try one more and I did *Conspiracies*. I had such fun writing and researching it (I went to UFO conventions) that I said, who am I kidding? I signed multi-book contracts from then on to do Repairman Jack novels. It hasn't been the only thing I've done since then, but he's pretty much taken over my writing career.

GF: *Do you miss the horror aspect of storytelling.*

FPW: The Jack novels have quite a bit of horror in them—very Lovecraftian. The typical Jack story is two pronged: a mundane problem plus the cosmic horror problem that's been dogging his life. So in the background there's the cosmic conflict that he's become entangled in. The irony of it is that here's this guy who's set up his entire life to be autonomous and he winds up having his strings pulled by these nameless, formless entities out there in space or in other dimensions; you're never quite sure where they are or whether you can pinpoint them. So there's a crime part and then there's a weird part that's influenced by Lovecraft's cosmic horror.

The series is coming to an end at number fifteen, and then it goes into *Nightworld,* which is the end of the Adversary Cycle. The Repairman Jack novels loop out from *The Tomb* and go around *The Touch* and *Reprisal* and then connect at *Nightworld*. It's laid out on the website in what I'm calling "The Secret History of the World." From pre-history to *Nightworld*.

GF: *Do you find the non-horror fans don't quite get the horror angle?*

FPW: Yes, and they complain about it on the website. "I really like Repairman Jack and the clever fixes, but what's this supernatural stuff going on?" It's usually not the other way around. Certain hardcore crime people find the supernatural stuff off-putting.

GF: *What do you think makes a series character successful?*

FPW: It's what makes any character successful. It's the same principle in a stand-alone book. You've got a fleshed-out guy that you can identify with, someone you want to come back to. It happens a lot in mysteries and thrillers. With Jack, I wanted a different kind of hero and I created what I consider an anti-Jason Bourne. He's not ex-CIA, or an ex-SEAL, no experience in Black-Ops, no special forces training, he can't go and call on his old buddies in the FBI or CIA when he needs something. He learned it all on the streets and in that sense, he's a real blue-collar hero. I wanted him to be the kind of guy you wouldn't mind sitting down and having a beer with. And the fact that he has no identity, that he's never had a social security number and he's never paid taxes, never had a legal driver's license—he has one but it's fake—puts him apart; there's really no other character like him, except maybe Vachss's Burke—but Jack came first. So Jack lives completely under the radar and people seem to find his anarchist streak and invisibility appealing.

GF: *What do you see as some of the pitfalls to writing a series?*

FPW: If you start with a series and it's successful, you're not going to be able to get away from it. And if that's all you do, then your whole reputation as a writer is going to be tied to that character. That's the danger. I did quite a few books before I started the series, and I made a point of doing a science fiction novel every so often, as well as side trips like *Midnight Mass* and the *Fifth Harmonic*. I've made a point to write outside Jack along the way to keep people aware that this isn't the only thing I do. That's the trap: being so identified with the character that you can't get away from him- or her. You can go to the extreme success like Sherlock Holmes where the readers wouldn't let Doyle kill him and made him bring Holmes back. Jack has nowhere near that popularity, but people do make faces when I announce there's only three more books in the series.

GF: *On the flipside, what are the benefits of a series character?*

FPW: You get to know him and also you don't have to invent someone new every time. You build up a circle of friends and acquaintances he can deal with. Jack has his friend Julio who owns the bar he frequents, his gun-runner friend Abe, who's extremely popular. People are hounding me on the website to do a series with Abe as hero, but Abe is anything but a leading man, so that'll never happen. And he's got his girlfriend Gia, who people have a mixed reaction to. There have actually been threads on the website about killing Gia. The women don't want her.

Surprisingly, half the readership is female. I looked at this as a guy's type of thing - 90% male. It's guns and horror and all sorts of action / thriller tropes. But on my last book tour, half the crowds were always women. They'd come to me and say how much they loved the guy. I guess I touched a nerve unconsciously. One woman said, "We're all looking for our white knight and it's hard to find him out there, so we'll take Jack until he comes along." I never thought of him as a white knight. I thought his armor would be very tarnished. I think his imperfections help. He makes mistakes and misjudgments; things go wrong and sometimes they're his fault. So in that sense he's very human and not this infallible super dude. If you're going to have supernatural elements, then you have to put extra effort into making everything else real - and screwing up is certainly part of everyone's reality.

GF: *Is it difficult after all these books to keep track of everything? Do you have a compendium?*

FPW: I wish I did. There's one in the works, but it won't be done in time to help me. I do have readers who seem to know everything. They like to go back and read them again and again, so they know so much more about what's going on than I do. Some people are really tuned in and I hope they stay that way, at least until I finish the series. They're my go-to guys.

GF: *It must be an awesome feeling to know that there are readers who know your books and characters as well as if not better than you do.*

FPW: It is. It's a little ... scary isn't the right word, but it is scary, that you've somehow tapped into the their psyche enough that they want to become that involved. I can remember being like that with certain writers like Lovecraft. I knew all the books and I was ready to apply to Miskatonic University. But it's strange to be on the receiving end. That again, is the strength of a series: that people really know the guy, book after book. After a while he becomes almost real to them.

GF: *Do you think a series is the best way to brand an author?*

FPW: No. King and Koontz did it without series characters, as did Ken Follett. I think if it's a really successful series, that'll help, but certainly movies brand-name you. There's nothing like a movie or television series to put you in the public's mind. Look at Jim Butcher. People were reading his books, but nothing like what they are now. Same with Charlaine Harris now. Sherilynn Kenyon and Laurell K Hamilton have managed to do it without movies. But they do have series.

GF: *Have you ever been swayed by a reader's suggestions?*

FPW: I discourage that on the website. People have said, Let's do fan fiction, and stuff like that, but it can be tough on me legally if I'm already thinking of something and someone proposes a similar idea on the website; it looks like I've cribbed from them. Basically, the arcs are pretty much set for the series, so that even if someone has a really good suggestion, it probably won't fit in. But I can always steal it for something else. People claim stolen property even when you don't steal from them.

GF: *What do you say to writers who want to write a series?*

FPW: It has its pros and cons. Do it under a different name if you're just starting out, and compartmentalize your work so that if the series doesn't work out, you can start over under your own name. Joe Konrath started out writing eight books that were never published. Then he landed a multi-book contract from Hyperion for a series with a female police detective, Jacqueline Daniels (known as Jack Daniels). And every book is named after a cocktail. But he's also coming out with a horror novel called *Afraid*, but he's doing it under the pen name of Jack Kilborn. That's another way to get around it. If you make your bones with your series, then you have credibility as a writer and editors will look at something new, outside the series. A different publisher took *Afraid*. That's one way to have your cake and eat it too. Nora Roberts did it as J. D. Robb. If you're going to do a series, be ready to switch to another name when you want to do something different. If you're writing a popular or reliable series where the publisher can count on a regular number of sales, they won't want you to break from the series.

GF: *Are publishers more forgiving time wise with authors who are writing a series in terms of a regular publishing schedule?*

FPW: No, just the opposite. Sometimes, when they're initiating a series, they want to put the books out every six months. In those cases they want you to have two or three in the can so they can put them out one right after the other. If you really want a career in commercial fiction, you have to be able to put out a book a year. When you don't have a series, and you sell well, the publisher's more forgiving. If you're trying to build a career, you really need to keep up a flow: the paperback reprint of the last hardcover released in, say, September, and then the new hardcover out in October. That way the paperback is out there containing an excerpt from the hardcover, which gooses the sales of the hardcover.

GF: *Do you think that if an author has a series going, when the new book comes out it helps the backlist more than an author with a bunch of stand alone titles?*

FPW: Absolutely. Ongoing success in this game is all about backlist. A recent Zogby survey showed that 89% of readers search for books by author - someone they've enjoyed before. Which is good for anyone's backlist. But if that first book was part of a series, the first thing they want is more of that series - and they want the *whole* series. When they exhaust the series, they may or may not move on to your other titles, but a series builds loyalty. The backlist is the whole purpose of the Amazon Shorts program. I don't know if it's still true, but at the start you had to have books for sale on Amazon before they'd take your short story. Why? Not for the 29 cents they net from each download. No, they want to drive readers to your backlist. During the program's first year and a half, my Repairman Jack piece, "The Long Way Home," was the most downloaded story (I'm talking fiction - non-fiction sells better there than fiction), and during that time I noticed an uptick in backlist sales. I donated a Jack story to the *Thriller* anthology (which turned out to be the best selling anthology in history) and I gained a lot of new readers from that. So having a series helps in other ways.

GF: *There you have it. The word on writing series characters from the guy who knows, F. Paul Wilson.*

CHAPTER 23

Tim Deal

It's All About the Work: An Interview with Tom Piccirilli

TIMOTHY DEAL has authored more than 100 published stories, news pieces, features, and analysis on topics related to technology, business, entertainment, the arts, and film. He is the publisher of *Shroud Magazine*, and the editor of three horror anthologies including the Bram Stoker Award-nominated *Beneath the Surface*. Tim currently sits as the Publications Chair for the New England Horror Writers executive committee.

TOM PICCIRILLI has sewn the seeds of his fiction within the fetid soil of the horror genre. With more than 20 published novels, the prolific and award-winning author of *Headstone City* and *The Midnight Road* has since bare-knuckled his way into crime fiction, garnering him both critical praise and a stalwart fan base. His writing is unforgiving and brutal, yet often incorporates the sympathetic themes of familial loyalty, heritage, and even love. Tom has more than 150 stories in print spanning the noir, mystery, horror, erotica, and science fiction genres. He has been a final nominee for the World Fantasy Award and has won the prestigious Bram Stoker Award for best novel in 2005, though he has been nominated several times.

Tim Deal: *Explain your personal process for approaching a new project, particu-*

larly a novel. How do you nurture the seed of an idea into fruition? Do you outline a novel first? Do you know how every project will end when you begin it, or does it take on a life of its own?

Tom Piccirilli: The process is very organic. It needs to be a journey of surprise and discovery for me, otherwise I don't really see the point of writing at all. I'm not just here to say something. I need to have something to say. And the only way for that to happen is to start the story and then see what new places it leads me. Once I'm on some new ground, in a different place, I have a new perspective. If my perspective weren't always shifting, I'd just be telling the same story over and over.

TD: *Can you lend some insight into your writing environment? What are your writing routines and nuances? Does your writing environment convey a sense of mood that befits or supports the tone of the project? Is there any item within your personal writing environment that you cannot write without?*

TP: I burn out easily in front of the empty page / empty screen. I'm in a constant need of refreshing myself, so I'll write for twenty minutes, and then go watch a movie. And I'll write for a half hour, and then I'll walk the dogs. I'll write, and then go read for a bit. Some authors will say that they write for four hours a day or write between the hours of two to six, but for me it's continuous. I'm always writing, even when I'm doing something else. That's the way it has to be for me. People ask that old chestnut question of where do you get your ideas. The ideas don't come to me in the chair in front of the screen. The ideas come while I'm out there doing what I do, being who I am, and then I bring them back to the desk. So the only real "items" I need are time to collect my thoughts and space to establish them.

TD: *How do you approach obstacles to a particular writing project? How do you reignite the creative process when/if it stalls? How do you move past mundane interruptions, unproductive moods, hungry pets, and other entities competing for your attention?*

TP: Two things keep me climbing up the mountain and over the molehills. First, I have a need to write. I'm not sure where it comes from except that the need to fantasize has always been with me. I need to take what I see, what I learn, what I think, and all the questions that I have about life, and mold all of that into a different form. We all need a mixture of the world as it is and the world as metaphor, as art. If we didn't, there would be no music, no plays, no film, no poetry, no literature. A fundamental part of the human condition is to take what we know of reality and reshape it, rethink it, reimagine it.

The other more mercenary aspect of the creative drive is that I pray to the great god mortgage. I need to pay my bills, and I do that only so long as I produce. So when the process stalls, I get it going again by any means necessary. Whether I have to sit at the screen for an hour rewriting the same paragraph or whether I need to talk with fellow writers or reread my favorite novels then that's what I'll do. The responsibilities of my life can only be attended to through my art. Some people think that writing for money—creating art for money—is selling out. But it's the opposite. It means walking the wire without a net. It means not being able to say, "I'll only create when inspiration finds me, and I'll go be an accountant or a computer programmer the other 29 days of the month." It means you have to go out and track your inspiration down and wrestle it to the floor every single day. That's not selling out your work. That's putting the greatest amount of faith in it. The roof over your head is at stake. The food in your mouth is at stake. Your very life is at stake.

TD: *What are some of the most important lessons you have learned about the craft of writing over the years? Is there anything that you do differently now than when you were a fledgling writer?*

TP: Control is the main thing. Not merely control of the writing but control of the themes I have, the recurring motifs that for whatever reason mean a great deal to me. It's a matter of distillation. You take your worldview and you distill it down onto the page. You learn over time what you're good at and what you're not. When your story is likely to jump the rails and when it's on track. You gain control of your own literary footing. Anyone can write a novel. Anyone can fill up the pages. Anyone can tell a story that unwinds, that unspools, that vomits, that clanks, that scratches. But only someone who's put the time in will discover where to grease the wheel, where to oil the hinge, where to hold back, where to let go. All of that isn't just control of story, it's control of yourself while you're telling the story. You discover how to keep yourself interested, eager, and curious where the material is concerned. In my early days I was all fire without control. I'd rub two sticks together and before I knew it I had a wildfire on my hands. Characters, events, mood, backstories, they'd all just come pouring out and I had no way to handle it. My work would get beyond my control. I'd lose my hold on it, and the work suffered because of it. Now I can hold onto it more tightly. I'm more aware of my own limitations and can play to my strengths.

TD: *As you have developed as a writer, you have transitioned from horror to crime fiction/noir. Explain the reasons/motivations for this transition?*

TP: As I started to slide over the hill of middle age it seemed that I became a lot more interested in dealing with authentic and realistic matters rather than fantastical ones. I had enough of my life already behind me to see the arch of where I'd been and where I was going. I could be a little more self-aware in my exploration of the work but still keep a lot of the same dramatic context that I'd always known. Crime fiction often deals with the average man gone bad. He approaches the line and for whatever reason tips over it. That was something I could certainly understand. The older one gets the worse those temptations grow, I think. You start thinking more about your own mortality. The average disappointments add up. The regular failings take on greater weight. So a small jump from horror to crime seemed in order.

Noir fiction can be as frightening and cold and illuminating as horror fiction can be. You're still dealing with the same forces of good versus evil. Crime seems to allow for more of a gray area between the black and the white. Horror demands certain extremes. By definition you need something horrific going on. So the distance between the good and bad is greater. In crime fiction the gap is often narrowed. Even in noir/hardboiled novels where the protagonist commits awful acts for his femme fatale honey, you know he's doing it for a human reason. He's trapped by the inevitability of his vice and his lust. He was fated to go on a downward slide from the onset. In horror, someone is fated to stand up. In noir, someone is fated to go down.

TD: *Are you writing with your audience in mind, or are you essentially writing to fulfill your own needs, or both? Is there a distinction?*

TP: Well, in a very real way it's the same thing. We are our own audience. We are always aware of ourselves. We say what we say and we can hear that echoing voice in our own heads. We hear ourselves. We view ourselves. So fulfilling the need as an artist is fulfilling the need of an audience, at least at one level.

So the question arises, How well do we know ourselves? How impressed with ourselves are we? Are you painting a picture with lots of blue in it because blue is your favorite color? Is that going to impress people who enjoy green and red as well? Again, the work has to take on a life of its own. The work has to become a separate entity that grows from what we feed it otherwise what's the point? Sometimes scenes will fall a different way from how I would like them to because I know the story will benefit for it. Sometimes I have to kill off beloved characters because the story needs for that to happen. I don't know if my reader will like it or hate it, but I feel that it needs to be done.

The thing is that "the audience" or "the reader" is singular. It makes it sound like there's only one person out there reading over your shoulder. One big group that's watching the performance. But it's not. It's many different people with many different tastes and preferences. There's no way to impress them all, so you try to aim your work toward one kind of person. The person who will enjoy the thing that you feel you need to do with your story.

TD: *What are the most important lessons you have learned about the BUSINESS of writing, selling your work, and managing your career?*

TP: I haven't learned anything about the business. It's well beyond my meager understanding. It is confusing and frustrating and goes against my personal grain. I don't know why the business side of things does what it does or falls the way it falls. The only rule I have is to protect the work. Don't just worry about getting published but worry about being published well. Deal with someone who will respect what you do. Who will respect all the time and sweat and energy and lonely hours you have given to the work.

CHAPTER 24

Michael Knost

It's All About the Craft: An Interview with Ramsey Campbell

MICHAEL KNOST is an author, columnist, and editor of horror, dark fiction, and supernatural thrillers. He has written books in various genres, edited anthologies such as the *Legends of the Mountain State* series, *Spooky Tales from Mountain State Writers, Appalachian Holiday Hauntings* (with Mark Justice), and *Bullets and Brimstone* (also with Mark Justice). Michael's latest novel, *To the Place I Belong,* will be published in 2010, and is a novel based on a haunted coalmine in Southern West Virginia. To find out more, visit www.MichaelKnost.com.

The *Oxford Companion to English Literature* describes RAMSEY CAMPBELL as "Britain's most respected living horror writer." He has been given more awards than any other writer in the field, including the Grand Master Award of the World Horror Convention, the Lifetime Achievement Award of the Horror Writers Association and the Living Legend Award of the International Horror Guild. Among his novels are *The Face That Must Die, Incarnate, Midnight Sun, The Count of Eleven, Silent Children, The Darkest Part of the Woods, The Overnight, Secret Story, The Grin of the Dark* and *Thieving Fear.* Forthcoming are *Creatures of the Pool* and *The Seven Days of Cain.* His collections include *Waking Nightmares, Alone with the Horrors, Ghosts and Grisly Things, Told by the Dead* and *Just Behind You,* and his non-fiction is collected as *Ramsey Campbell, Probably.*

His novels *The Nameless* and *Pact of the Fathers* have been filmed in Spain. His regular columns appear in *All Hallows, Prism, Dead Reckonings* and *Video Watchdog*. He is the President of the British Fantasy Society and of the Society of Fantastic Films. Ramsey lives on Merseyside with his wife Jenny. His pleasures include classical music, good food and wine, and whatever's in that pipe. His web site is at www.ramseycampbell.com.

Michael Knost: *Why horror?*

Ramsey Campbell: Lovecraft declared that the weird tale—by which he meant much of what I mean by horror fiction—could only ever be a portrayal of a certain type of human mood. Certainly one of the pleasures of some of the greatest work in the field is the aesthetic experience of terror (which involves appreciating the structure of the piece and, in prose fiction, of the selection of language). I don't see this as limited. There's surely no more reason to criticise a piece for conveying only this experience than there is to object to a comedy for being nothing except funny (as might be said of Laurel and Hardy, surely the greatest exponents on film) or a tragedy for making its audience weep. Indeed, I wish more of the field still assailed me with dread: these days little besides the darker films of David Lynch achieve it. How ever, the field is capable of much more, and frequently succeeds—as satire or as comedy (however black), as social comment, as psychological enquiry, and perhaps best of all when it aspires to the awesome, the sense of something larger than can be directly shown. One reason I stay in the field is that I haven't found its boundaries.

MK: *What story or book are you most proud of writing?*

RC: At the moment I'm quite taken with *The Grin of the Dark*, but there's never any knowing how long my liking for a recent book of mine will last.

I continue to be fond of *Needing Ghosts,* and it may be significant that I'd call them both nightmare comedies. As a collection *Alone with the Horrors* is pretty good, I think.

MK: *Reading other writers who are establishing themselves as solid up-and-comers, do you occasionally see something that reminds you of your own writing? If so, who?*

RC: I must admit I'd feel presumptuous to claim that I've influenced anyone. There are certainly writers who say that I have, but I wouldn't assume it without being told.

MK: *How does it feel to know you have influenced a good number of successful writers?*

RC: It feels fine, because if I'm anything as a writer, I think I'm a link in a tradition. I've learned from writers as diverse as Lovecraft and M. R. James and Leiber on the one hand, Nabokov and Graham Greene on the other. I think continuity is very valuable—crucial, even. That isn't to say that great originality is impossible, but it must have a foundation in what precedes it too.

MK: *If you had three books to offer a twelve-year-old in hopes of converting him- or her into a reader, what would the three titles be?*

RC: Lord! They might never forgive me. I'll suggest Philip Pullman's *His Dark Materials* trilogy, Ray Bradbury's *The Martian Chronicles* (or the title I prefer, *The Silver Locusts*) and *Brighton Rock.* They would work for me (well, two did, but then I was already long converted).

MK: *What is your biggest pet peeve in writing?*

RC: People who bugger about with my text, especially if they haven't even the courtesy to ask if I agree to changes.

MK: *What is the best advice you could give someone who thinks he or she is ready to write full time?*

RC: If you can't make a living doing it—that is, if your writing isn't already earning you a significant income—then it's a crazy idea. Then again, it's one I had after only two published books, and I followed it into the unknown. My wife supported me for years; otherwise I strongly suspect you wouldn't be hearing from me now. Still, writers are crazy, and nothing any other writer says is likely to change them.

CHAPTER 25

Lucy A. Snyder

It's All Part of the Fun: An Interview with Clive Barker

LUCY A. SNYDER frequently escaped into Clive Barker's worlds when she was in darkest academia pursuing her MA in journalism. She is the author of *Sparks and Shadows, Installing Linux on a Dead Badger,* and the forthcoming Del Rey novel *Spellbent.* Her writing has appeared in publications such as *Strange Horizons, Farthing, Masques V, Doctor Who Short Trips: Destination Prague, Chiaroscuro, GUD, Legends of the Mountain State* 2, and *Lady Churchill's Rosebud Wristlet.* You can learn more about her at www.lucysnyder.com.

CLIVE BARKER represents one of popular fiction's rarest combinations, a bestselling author who is also praised by his peers as a highly talented writer in the tradition of Henry James and Edgar Allan Poe. He began writing short stories while running the London theater company he founded at the age of 21. His six-volume collection *Books of Blood* includes dozens of these unflinchingly grotesque stories, many of which have been adapted as horror movies. After early disappointments with some of these adaptations, Barker began adapting and directing his own work. Among his best-known films are the *Hellraiser* series and *Candyman* and its sequel.

If you've sought out *Writers Workshop of Horror,* you already know Clive Barker's name. In fact, you probably own at least one of his many books or movies. But just in case you've stumbled upon this after having been trapped in a 1983 time bubble, or if you've recently returned from two decades on a remote, incommunicado island in the South Pacific, read on. You'll learn much more about the man of whom Stephen King once said, "I have seen the future of horror and his name is Clive Barker."

Barker was born in Liverpool, England in 1952, and led himself into storytelling at a young age. "There were double-doors at the back of our yard. In England a yard is typically just a paved area, no grass, perhaps ten feet by ten feet with a high wall around it. Ours was like the yard I describe in *Weaveworld.* The double-doors led onto the alleyway and opened inwards. And so I was able to put a little puppet theatre there. And over three or four summers starting when I was 8, I was able to put on afternoon shows twice a week, and perhaps have six or seven people in my alleyway audience to watch some self-invented tale of ghosts and things that go bump in the night."

He began writing fiction just a few years later. "The best of those stories are in *The Adventures of Mr. Maximillian Bacchus and His Travelling Circus,* which have been published with amazing illustrations by Richard Kirk. It's exciting because I started these stories when I was in my teens and finished them in my twenties. There are only four of them, and they're very short, but I tinkered with them and tinkered with them, and then I didn't do anything with them at the end of it all. But now I have done something with them, and finally they'll come out."

Barker says that he did relatively little revision on the *Bacchus* stories before he delivered them to Bad Moon Books. "Obviously I think you can't get back to where you were then, and the last time I touched this truly was over 30 years ago. And to amend it, frankly, would be untrue to who I was when I wrote it."

He's not certain how readers are going to react to this look into the still-budding imagination of a very young Clive Barker. "I don't have the slightest clue. And actually that's part of the fun of it, of course," he says.

"My influences are very obvious in *Bacchus*. And some will be surprising to some people; others may be obscure, like Lord Dunsany, for instance. He's a fantasist from the 19th Century, and there are extraordinary stories by him. They'll be three or four pages long, beautiful, beautiful little jewels. He dove into the fantastical element of his narrative from the first sentence. And obviously, because the stories are so short, that it's a necessary element of his style, which I loved and learned from," Barker says.

"And Coleridge is a very obvious influence because the circus ends up going to Xanadu: 'In Xanadu did Kublai Khan a stately pleasure dome decree.' They take this as literally the truth and they head off as per Coleridge's instructions. So I'm wearing my literary influences on my sleeve in the book. Much more than perhaps I would do now, which isn't to say that those influences aren't there now, but a fledgling writer perhaps is less likely to obscure them, maybe even likes to show them off. I was a young guy and I loved Coleridge, and I loved Yeats, and I loved circuses. So, I have no idea how people will read it, but I hope kindly."

As a young man, Barker also wrote plays for local theatre groups, and he says that the experience helped him tremendously. "Making plays makes you very aware of your responsibility to your audience in a way that really no other medium does, even cinema. Because you sit in an audience and you're very aware of when you've lost them. When you're boring them. When you're irritating them. When you're horrifying them. When you're making them laugh. You become very aware of your responsibility and that's informed my writing ever since."

He says that he routinely reads his work aloud to himself. "It's a lesson I learned from one of Joseph Conrad's letters. Reading aloud would be his way to discover where the errors were, where the echoes were, where the cadences were wrong, and I've found that to be absolutely wonderful advice, and I always do it however lengthy the books become."

And some of his books have been quite lengthy; *Weaveworld* and *The Great and Secret Show* are each close to 700 pages in paperback. But he's got tremendous creative breadth as well. Ever since he made a huge splash with the *Books of Blood* and *The Hellbound Heart* in the mid-80s, Barker has written more than 25 novels and story collections along with several books of plays, essays and poetry. He has created thousands of paintings, and has written four movies, directed three, and produced eight others.

Given the extent of his creative output, you would be correct if you guessed that Barker adheres to a fairly strict work schedule.

"Every day is a writing day," he says. "I get to my desk between 8 and 8:30 in the morning and then work through until 6pm, and then normally I'll take up whatever will be happening in the evening, usually painting or photography."

When he's engrossed in the initial drafts of a new novel, Barker writes at least 2,000 words each and every day. "I do about four drafts total. I do handwritten drafts because I don't type and I have no wish to type. I mean, I know how to type, but I have no interest in putting the words down that way."

Barker writes in pen (usually Pentels) on loose leaf, college-ruled paper. "Maybe that's because I'm an artist and because I've always used a pen and so there's a sort of natural feel to it. I don't know how familiar you are with Blake's illuminated texts, but you know very often he'll literally make words flower. It's really this glorious thing in bringing words and pictures into the same place, the same space."

As he reaches the later drafts, his work style changes. "There's a little shift of gears in a way, because writing requires, particularly when it's final polish, real attention to every last detail of colon and semicolons and so on. And when I get into the painting phase in the evenings, sometimes I suspend the analytical part of my head and let instinct take over as I paint, whether I'm working with oils or as now with sumi ink and oil pastel. I'm really giving myself almost entirely over to instinct."

Barker says that each of his projects has its own unique demands. "I'm writing the third book in the *Abarat* quintet. So this is the lynchpin book, the book that stands at the very center of the balancing act. We've established all the characters, we've established all the drama, now we are going to move into the scale of the battles and the confrontation and the secrets and the dynasties within dynasties and the worlds within worlds, which is something I've always played with. And this is a book of revelations, really. It's a bit of a tough book to write because I'm holding a lot of information in my head at the same time, not only about what I've already written in the first two books, but also about what I know is going to happen and the clues that are being left in those books which are now going to start to bear fruit in the books to come."

Barker does most of his writing on a huge wooden table. "It's five by eight, I think. I have a lectern in front of me, and on it I have the typed-out text plus various notes and things that have to go into pages. I'm at the point where I'm making marks on the typed pages that someone else has transcribed from my fourth handwritten draft, and now I'm making a final pass on that text."

His penultimate and ultimate drafts often involve adding considerable amounts of new material. If you take a look at one of the printouts on his lectern, you're likely to see a dense mass of black-ink strikeouts and penned additions crowding every margin and almost obscuring the original triple-spaced san-serif print. "Dickens used to go into galleys and transform his manuscripts at that stage, and it drove his publishers crazy. If I could do that, I would!" he laughs.

"But HarperCollins isn't going to let me do that. The very last time that I can really *seriously* screw around with things is now. And I want to make this the best thing I can. I feel hugely indebted to my audience, to my readers, for being with me through not a particularly simple journey, in that I first started out writing short horror fiction with a large erotic content which was difficult I think for some people, particularly when it was homoerotic content, and then I wrote fantasy for a long time. And then just as people were just starting to get used to the idea of me writing these large, fantastical tomes with a lot of violence and sexuality in them and hopefully philosophy as well, and then I go off and start writing for children.

"But readers have come with me, and it's so glorious that I can now go to signings, and those people will come with their own children. Someone will say, 'This is my daughter, and she's five, and I'm reading her *The Thief of Always*, which my mum gave to me sixteen years ago.' I'm Italian and Irish and my feelings run close to the surface, and that's the kind of thing that will make me need to go to the restroom and wipe the tears out of my eyes.

"I'm constantly trying to make what Stephen King called head movies or skull movies: things should be playing out on the inside of your eyes, if you will, without you having to think about me as an author being present. I have no interest in being present, in intervening between you and the work. My job is to be as invisible as possible. My job is to say, 'Hey, I wrote this book and I'm on the cover, bye bye!' The story should have its own momentum; it should make its own way. I have no patience for that showy kind of writing, which is all about how clever the writer is. Postmodern stuff just leaves me totally cold. I'm much more interested in being drawn into a book, and I want to create the kind of writing which hopefully makes you turn and turn the pages."

Unlike writers such as Stephen King and Peter Straub, Barker has no interest in co-authoring novels or stories. "I write because I'm on my own. I write because there's a purity to the act. I do painting the same way. I have no interest whatsoever in writing with somebody else. Not because

I don't hugely admire other writers, I do, but that's one of the reasons I wouldn't want to do it."

However, Barker is perfectly happy to collaborate with other creators in other media. He's worked with other artists and writers in adapting his work into the *Tortured Souls* collectible figures series and into comics and graphic novels, video games, and of course movies. "Film is even more collaborative than theatre in a way, because I do sort of roughly know how to do everybody's jobs in the theatre. But if it were just me and a camera, I couldn't make a film if my life depended on it."

He's focused on constantly growing as a creator. "I think for a writer every day is sort of unexplored territory. I think every day you are going where you haven't gone before. If you've been there before, why are you there? What are you doing telling a story you've already told?"

Although Barker's work has evolved beyond his horror roots, some readers have apparently wanted more of his early work, resulting in many of them not seeming to understand what he has tried to achieve in his more recent novels.

"I made a huge mistake," he says of his 2007 novel *Mister B. Gone*, lamenting that he'd inadvertently primed his audience to anticipate a book in the vein of *The Hellbound Heart*. "I should *never* have made the creature a demon. I should have done something that didn't lay that expectation into the text. I was horribly disappointed by reader reactions. It was a book that means a lot to me. It was a comedic book; a dark one, certainly, but essentially a comedy. A comedy of how we come to be human, or fail to. And I certainly enjoyed writing it, it was just a lovely experience. And to find so many readers saying 'Why can't he just give us the *Books of Blood* again?' ... that was the *cri du coeur*, you know, it really was the essence of the complaint of people who didn't like it. Their objection was that I was writing horror again but I wasn't writing it the way I used to," he says.

"Well, of *course* I wasn't writing it the way I used to! The *Books of*

Blood were 25 years ago. I'm a different human being now, you know? I don't *want* to write it the way I used to write. I have no interest in doing that. That would be tiresome and boring, and I think it would be boring for them, too."

In addition to *Mister B. Gone,* he says that *Coldheart Canyon* is the other book that has been the most poorly received by readers. "They're both books which don't do what people expected them to. *Coldheart Canyon* has a lot more very twisted sex, more than people were comfortable with. I got a lot of objections about that from readers that I thought would be *way* over that kind of thing, and I was shocked that they were uncomfortable with it," he laughs.

"So you can't please all the people all the time. All you can do is what pleases *you,* and hope that it pleases other people. I love my readers, and I respect my readers, but I'm not going to simplify or echo myself, copy myself, just so the sales will be better."

He found his first model for forging his own path in Lord Dunsany's work. "He'll start with 'The goblin on the rocket'—I'm making this specific example up—'threw down his five-fingered pipe and cried to the gods.' And you just have to go, 'Oh, okay'. You either buy it or you don't buy it. And there's something very defiant about that, which I *love.*

"The first paragraph of *Imagica* is impenetrable, and it's designed to be so. It's sort of, 'I dare you. Go on. Read it,'" Barker laughs. "It's like saying, 'Either be up for this, or don't be.' It's the reverse of what Tolkien very cannily does at the beginning of *The Lord of the Rings.* Which is to introduce a massive and very violent epic in which women and love really have no place with a rather jolly rural scene, complete with an avuncular wizard, who turns out not to be avuncular at all, but actually is sort of a massive, almost divine force for good. And it's a fake-out, you know? Those first hundred pages or so are absolutely not representative of what the book is."

Barker has arranged his life to fuel his creativity and productivity.

By day, he keeps his neurons firing with a steady stream of English breakfast tea. But his work doesn't stop at night; he keeps a dream journal close at hand.

"The term 'dream journal' might be misleading in the sense that while of course I dream every night, I don't always remember my dreams. But when I remember my dreams I write them down," he says. "The term 'dream journal' maybe implies that I'm actively pursuing an examination of my dreams or something like that. And I'm not. I'm simply recording them when they come along. For instance, at the end of each of the *Abarat* books is a very simple, usually rather oblique poem. The *Abarat* books are littered with poems of various kinds, and very often they're short and anonymous. I didn't have anything for the end of *Abarat 3*, and it's troubled me.

"Three nights ago, I had the page in front of me, a barely-legible scrawl because I was nearly asleep, but I wrote:

Night comes down upon my heart
and smothers me in grief.

Let us take comfort before we part
for at least our lives are brief.

"I don't have the first clue where that came from, but that's the wonderful thing about the dreaming experience because you *don't* know where it comes from, and it is a mystery. And now this poem is going at the end of the book."

Barker has thought about the literary legacy he hopes to leave behind. "In the grand metaphysical scheme of things, I think that Jung was right and Freud was wrong: the collective unconscious is in our daily lives. And in *The Great and Secret Show* and in *Everville* I call it Quiddity, the dream sea where human imagination is floating. In the *Abarat* books it's 25 islands, each a different hour of the day plus one. Each a concentration of what the human psyche is putting into that particular hour, how we feel at midnight is so different than we feel at 3 in the afternoon. So I'm constantly trying to track the journeys that our psyches take.

"I would like to be erased as an individual; my history as a human being is not of any great interest. What I would like to think is that I've enriched the flotsam and jetsam that float on the sea of our unconscious."

CHAPTER 26

Jack M. Haringa

The Agnotology of Horror; or, Lies the Internet Told You

JACK M. HARINGA is a freelance writer and proofreader, and the co-editor of *Dead Reckonings*, a review journal of horror, dark fantasy, and suspense fiction. He also serves on the board of advisors to the Shirley Jackson Awards, which are given in recognition of outstanding achievement in the literature of psychological suspense, horror, and the dark fantastic. He teaches English in Worcester, Massachusetts, where he lives with his family.

The aspiring horror writer labors in a landscape that feels hostile to his- or her endeavors; it is a setting that appears composed of declining readership, growing anti-intellectualism, reorganizing publishers, folding magazines, and withering advances. Of even greater detriment to beginning authors is the virtual avalanche of bad advice and misinformation that roars over their screens each time they go on-line, from suggestions that established authors are trying to hold down new writers to the idea that giving away stories to websites in exchange for exposure will actually help one's career. Those who neither write well nor publish well are, unfortunately, staples of both online forums and the shadowy fringes of many writers' conventions, and their advice is as abundant as it is useless.

With a little effort, a lot of active reading, and a healthy skepticism toward the suggestions of those who perpetrate common mistakes, new writers can break the bonds of Internet-induced ignorance and begin crafting literate, saleable stories. Forthwith I offer five rules for the beginning writer designed to help them dodge the pitfalls that set my teeth on edge as a reader, teacher, reviewer, and editor.

The Lie: *Worrying about every word is for that snobby "literary" fiction.*

The Rule: *Know what words mean.* This seems obvious, but you would be astounded at the lack of control over vocabulary that many beginning writers evince in their work. Words have meanings, both denotative—according to the dictionary—and connotative—according to their cultural and societal weight. Many words have multiple meanings. When you use a word, be sure that it actually means what you think it means. A whisper, for instance, is not the same as a hiss. And if you claim that a character hisses his dialogue, said dialogue had better include a bunch of sibilants. If it doesn't, you've used the wrong word. Using the wrong word is not clever or funny unless you're putting it in the mouth of your version of Mrs. Malaprop; otherwise, it makes you look a fool to the editor, and more than one of this type of error is enough to get your work summarily rejected. Remember that you are not Lewis Carroll's Humpty Dumpty; words don't mean what you choose them to mean.

There are more frequent errors of this type, often listed in style guides under the heading of commonly confused words. Using "imply" for "infer," "effect" for "affect," and "lay" for "lie" all fall into this category. Don't confuse "then" for "than" and know when to use "that," "which," and "who" (and then master the proper use of "whom" and "whose", which is not the same as "who's," no matter the sound). Closely related words have similar meanings but not the same meanings: "barely" is not a synonym for "nearly," for example. Just try substituting one for the other in your story and see where it gets you. "Robert was nearly eaten by a zombie" both makes sense and keeps your character alive. "Robert was barely eaten by a zombie" leaves you with a protagonist who is a little bit dead. Or maybe the zombie only just managed to finish the protagonist to the last drop; in any event, it's a sentence rendered absurd by a misused word. This should also serve as a caveat for the inveterate thesaurus user: not all synonyms are created equal, and a thesaurus is not a dictionary. If you are using such a reference to find a substitute because you want to avoid repetition (a laudable endeavor), make certain the synonym you've chosen has precisely the meaning you need. Words are the most basic tools in the writer's toolkit. If an author can't be bothered to know how words work, it's unlikely said author will be producing anything worth reading.

The Lie: *Following the rules of grammar is outdated/ unimportant/ limiting to your creativity. Readers know what you mean. Besides, grammar is the editor's job.*

The Rule: *Know how words work together*. There are two meanings to this bit of advice. On the one hand, I'm talking about grammar. I recognize that this subject strikes fear into the hearts of many, triggering PTSD-like flashbacks of eighth grade English class and arcane rules about the subjunctive mood. Honestly, grammar isn't that difficult to understand. As I frequently tell my students, grammar is the skeleton on which we hang the flesh of language, and in the crafting of fiction it is also the sturdy framework that protects a story's heart and brain—its emotional effects and its deeper themes. Broken bones take the player out of the game; in the parlance of writing, awkwardly constructed and ill-conceived sentences break the readers' immersion in the story, reminding them that they are performing the task of reading something, and that this something isn't terribly well constructed. Your best bet, if you find yourself grammatically challenged, is to acquire a good text or style guide written for adults, and I frequently recommend books such as Patricia T. O'Conner's *Woe Is I* or Karen Elizabeth

Gordon's *The Deluxe Transitive Vampire* to students and writers alike. And please, don't buy into the defense of bad grammar as some kind of stylistic choice. Bad writers are quick to trot out Henry Miller, Ernest Hemingway, James Joyce, Cormac McCarthy and any number of other excellent writers as examples of people who break grammatical guidelines. While it is true that these authors did not always follow the conventions of standard grammar, they diverged from these conventions consciously, not accidentally. They knew the rules before they broke them, and they had a reason to break them in the precise way they did. It wasn't because they didn't know a gerund from an infinitive, and a new writer's mistakes will stand out as just that to any editor worth the title.

The other side of this rule connects directly with my first point. English offers a vast and varied vocabulary to its practitioners, and amongst its many choices are the idiomatic, two- and three-word verbs. Also known as phrasal verbs, these structures consist of, usually, a verb and a preposition (or two) working together to create a single and non-literal meaning. The humble verb "look" provides a long list of examples: we can look at, look over, look into, look through, look up, look after, look forward to, or look down on, and each action is significantly different due to the change in preposition. I have noticed a trend in recent years, however, of writers being unaware of the correct preposition meant to follow certain verbs either in phrase or in grammatical construction. Despite popular usage by sportscasters, radio personalities, or bloggers, you cannot base *off*, center *around*, or focus *in*; these days, learning grammar from broadcasters or other public figures is as reliable as learning it from rock lyrics. And from that you can't get no satisfaction.

The Lie: *You should use common familiar language everyone recognizes, and the most successful genre stories are built on tropes and archetypes.*

The Rule: *Know what makes a cliché a cliché.* This rule is about both the use of language and the construction of story; on both the microscopic and macroscopic levels, clichés present a danger to the new writer. The fact is that most of us speak in a combination of clichéd language and original phrasing. Clichés can function as a sort of conversational shorthand, like describing a person by comparing him to an actor. Neither of these things should be done in the writing of fiction. Conversation is ephemeral; people forget the common and banal phrasing of a discussion easily, retaining content over expression (most of the time). But when you commit cliché to paper, it gains a level of permanence that allows, even encourages, a reader to revisit its shopworn failure of originality, its laziness of expression, its cumbersome triteness, its creative bankruptcy, again and again. It would be my great pleasure to never again encounter something in a horror story that is pitch black, possessing inky depth, cold as the grave, or glinting like cold steel. I am exhausted at the very mention of "unspeakable horrors," of the encounter that "sent a chill up his spine," of the woman who "realizes the screams she hears are her own," of places that "filled him with dread," and of decisions that "made her wish she'd never been born." And that, to run afoul of a cliché, is just the tip of the iceberg. If you find yourself writing any of those phrases, stop, delete, and try again.

Story clichés, too, seem endemic to horror, both in fiction and in film, and they suggest that the writers don't read widely or deeply. In fact clichés could be considered a sort of extreme form of imitation, an unprocessed regurgitation of the most obvious aspects of shallow reading practices. But don't conflate the tropes of the genre—or the archetypes of our collective unconscious—with the clichés of bad horror. A vampire is not a cliché; it's a trope. A vampire who dresses in velvet suits and mopes through a story lamenting his loneliness and inability to die is a cliché, and a pretty exhausted one at that. And while it's true that some people build whole careers out of wringing every last drop of blood from such a turnip, the odds are much greater that an editor running into such a clichéd representation is just going to stamp it "been there, done that" and toss the submission in the circular file.

Wide reading, reading beyond the genre and beyond the contemporary, will aid a beginning writer in avoiding the first type of cliché. Broader exposure to good writers using language in various and original ways can help you start making the same kinds of connections. Also, stop reading bad books. It took me to the age of thirty to really internalize this rule, but ultimately I had to admit to myself that there were just too many good books I wasn't going to get to as it was, so I certainly shouldn't be wasting my time with work that is poorly written or empty. Add to your out-of-category exploration a deep reading of the horror genre itself to avoid the story cliché. Horror didn't start with Stephen King; Lovecraft and Poe aren't the only gothic writers who preceded him; and great horror novels don't always have the word "horror" on the spine. Good editors are well read, and they'll recognize when you're hoeing a well-worn row. See what's been done and do something different, or at least do a similar thing better. And if you ever find yourself seriously considering ending a story with a character realizing "it was all a dream," shut down the computer and go sign up for a trade that doesn't involve the creative use of language.

The Lie: *Analyzing what you read sucks the fun out of it, and besides, there aren't really any rules to what makes a good story.*

The Rule: *Know why stories work.* When you read, you should reflect on why a story or novel was or wasn't satisfying to you. Examine its elements: character, plot, setting, mood, point of view, theme. How do they fit together? Why and how did the character change over the course of the tale? (Change—growth or some other kind of development—in a character is essential in stories that involve conflict. And if your story doesn't contain conflict, it's likely not much of a story.) What did the author do to get the effects of the story? These are essential questions, and too often new writers separate their writing process from their reading experience. Every story—even a bad one—is a lesson spread before you. Raymond Chandler revealed that he learned plotting by taking apart every story of Earle Stanley Gardner's he could and rewriting it with new characters and settings. Note that he never tried to pawn these slavish plot imitations off as original material to the magazines; he was interested in how Gardner—a master plotter—was able to set things in motion and bring them to an effective conclusion. While this seems like a fairly extreme method, even a less methodical approach to one's reading can nonetheless afford one access to the mechanics of successful storytelling.

Knowing how stories work in part involves determining two essential facts: when the story should start, and when it should end; in technical terms, the writer needs to know how much exposition and how much denouement the story should contain. Beginning writers frequently start their stories either too late or too soon. In the horror genre, they are often instructed to begin their tales *in media res*, but if their first chapter begins in the midst of action and then they spend three chapters in a row in a flashback to fill the reader in on the characters and situation, they've made a serious error. The book started too late. The same may be said for short stories on a smaller scale. In the other direction, if your short story about the final showdown between a wild west ghost hunter and "the wraith what killed his pa" begins with the protagonist's first birthday, chances are you've started too soon. Endings, too, require varying degrees of gradation, from gentle unwinding to abrupt stops. Consider the level of ambiguity you wish to achieve, the number of loose ends that need braiding, the emotional resonance with which you might leave the reader when determining the length of the story's closing. And let's see if we can put a stop to the "but the horror continues..." sorts of final scenes—don't take your writing cues from *Friday the 13th, A Nightmare on Elm Street*, or, well, pretty much every American horror film of the last two decades. We're back in cliché territory again.

The Lie: *Plot is everything; genre writers don't think about classroom stuff like style and theme. That's for the snobby critics to figure out.*

The Rule: *Know what your story is about.*

At the end of the day, if you want people to remember your story after they've closed the book, magazine, or browser, it has to have been about something. This doesn't mean plot—plots are a dime a dozen, and if you want to be really reductive there's a pretty short list of them in the first place. But themes are a different matter. The theme is what the work says about the human condition. Theme is the point. It's what you have to say about the world through the telling of your story. As Colin Wilson once wrote, "no amount of verbal pyrotechnics are a substitute for having something to say;" and I'd suggest that no number of plot convolutions or "cool" set pieces in your story will make up for a lack of something to say, either. Think of how ultimately unsatisfying so many action and horror films are when you take the time to step back and realize that they consist merely of a series of scenes, perhaps with great special effects or creepy atmospherics, that don't add together to any real point or with any real characters and are strung together by a plot meant simply to propel the viewer from one tableau to the next. There is no shortage of genre stories with the same essential problem, filled with sound and fury, signifying nothing.

At a panel during a recent Northeastern Writers' Convention (Necon), the point was made that, if a writer couldn't say any more to describe what his- or her story was about than a recitation of plot, then the story was a failure. In other words, if one can't say more about one's tale than "it's about zombies," the story isn't much of a story at all. The most common counter-argument to this idea comes in the description of a writer's work as "pure entertainment." Out comes Sam Goldwyn's old chestnut, "If you want to send a message, call Western Union," used without understanding the context of political and social message films to which the studio head referred. Ultimately, this is an empty argument. The fact of the matter is that readers, like anyone else, care about stories when those stories say something relevant, interesting, or even revealing about their own lives and the world around them. This is especially true about editors, who tend to be more critical and demanding readers than average. Even books that appear to be the purist escapism, if they last, have at their hearts something more profound than a toy box-collision of plastic boogeymen. Think about what you, as a writer, want to say. Consider not just the *what* of your story, but the *why*. Being able to answer such a question marks the difference between the amateur and the professional.

A few last words about lies and misinformation. Horror succeeds on the strength of its metaphors, whether it be vampires as a symbol of sexual desire and the consequences of id unhampered by super-ego, or the scientist's creature run amok as a representation of technology unrestrained by morality or ethics, or the lumbering undead as a warning about the mindless state of consumerism. Horror writers succeed through the use of these metaphors in well-written, well-constructed, and moving stories that avoid cliché and reach for depth. Quality wins out, and poor work gets rejected. There is no cabal of established authors with a stranglehold on the publishing industry; such stories are paranoid fantasies concocted by the incompetent to excuse their failures. There is no profit in editors' refusing to publish new voices due to elitism or cronyism; editors have standards of quality, the application of which is their primary job because good stories sell more magazines and anthologies than bad ones. Write well. Learn from your mistakes. New writers don't like to hear the truth that stories get rejected for two main reasons: they've been submitted to the wrong market or they're not good enough. It's the latter statement that can be the hardest to accept, but it's the most important to understand. Write better.

CHAPTER 27

Robert N. Lee

How Stephen King's Writing Advice Broke My Heart and Smashed My Dreams

ROBERT N. LEE spent the beginning of his life in Vietnam, grew up all over the continental and other US, and has the requisite CV of spectacular and varied employment to be a much better and more dedicated writer, probably. He primarily works as a designer, but writes and publishes fiction and non-fiction from time to time, and co-edited the Hellbound Books anthology *Damned Nation* with David T. Wilbanks. His favorite band is Joy Division, his favorite movie is *Vanishing Point*, his favorite novel is *Watchmen*. He has two dogs, two cats, two kids—a boy and girl, each—and a fiancée he loves very much, and is getting used to living in Florida.

STEPHEN KING was born in Portland, Maine in 1947, the second son of Donald and Nellie Ruth Pillsbury King. He made his first professional short story sale in 1967 to Startling Mystery Stories. In the fall of 1973, he began teaching high school English classes at Hampden Academy, the public high school in Hampden, Maine. Writing in the evenings and on the weekends, he continued to produce short stories and to work on novels. In the spring of 1973, Doubleday & Co., accepted the novel *Carrie* for publication, providing him the means to leave teaching and write full-time. He has since published over 40 books and has become one of the world's most successful writers. Stephen lives in Maine and Florida with his wife, novelist Tabitha King. They are regular contributors to a number of charities including many libraries and have been honored locally for their philanthropic activities.

"King is a great writer because he lets it all hang out. His hopes and sentiments, his awful bitterness, those wounds that never heal and those scars across his body and psyche which he cannot help but count and re-count more frequently than he counts his millions, his essential kindness, his outrageous inferiority complex vis-a-vis contemporary American realism and its publishing infrastructure, it's all there on the page. He doesn't care whether or not he lives or dies, not in the sense we are discussing now, and he wouldn't care even if he wasn't the world's most popular writer. Under another set of circumstances, S. King would still be the barstool intellectual and substitute teacher who writes a novel every six months and throws it out; he just married someone who didn't dig the manuscripts out of the trash. He would write this stuff for free, as he himself has said."—Nick Mamatas

For the June 1983 issue, Stephen King gave an interview to *Playboy* in which I read possibly the worst piece of writing advice of my life, which I naturally took to heart. Almost twenty years later, in his one book dedicated to the subject, *On Writing,* King would admit that he was doing a lot of cocaine at the time, understandably prone to making up yarns for interviews, and this was one of them: that he wrote for eight hours every day except Christmas, the Fourth of July, and his birthday.

That *destroyed* me as a teenager, when I tried to write seriously for the first time. I could not live up to it, and it tortured me endlessly, this impossible ideal, what you would have to do to be a writer: do it like a nine to five job. I finally gave up in frustration, knowing I could never be a real writer, and did not take up writing again until my thirties, when I began to publish fiction and non-fiction.

I hated Stephen King—and I mean personally, like he'd hit me in the face or kicked my dog—for about a day after I read *On Writing.* How dare he? All those days I'd sat around with a typewriter, kicking myself because I couldn't do this job like it was plumbing or accounting, and *neither could he.* He made it up! He ruined my life.

Of course, King didn't really make me stop writing in my late teens, and ceasing the practice didn't ruin my life in any sense. It just meant I had time and energy to do a lot of other things, and some of them were very pleasant and some as personally rewarding as any writing I've published since.

I stopped because I became convinced—correctly, I think—that I had nothing to say. I hadn't read enough, hadn't done enough, hadn't learned enough. My attempts at writing fiction were all over the map, stylistically, but they shared two qualities: they were trite and they were stolen. When I was fifteen I wrote like King and Harlan Ellison. When I was sixteen I wrote like Lovecraft. When I was seventeen, I wrote like J.G. Ballard. I even tried a story imitating Shirley Jackson, once. They are all gone forever, thank God, but I miss that one least.

You can see it in my taking that nonsense about punching a clock in your home office so seriously: I didn't want to be a writer. I wanted to be Stephen King, and not even Stephen King, really, but a fantasy version of Stephen King based on Stephen King's fantasy version of himself, as it turned out. (You may pause for a moment to breathe if I just blew your mind.)

So I was mad for a day, as I said, and then realized that was stupid and I wasn't mad anymore. Because by then I'd learned for myself the big secret—or *my* big secret, anyway—about writing King didn't drop in that interview: do it how you do. Do it as often as you do, do it as hard as you do, do it where you do, do it when you do. If you are going to be an occasional writer, be that. If you are going to try earnestly to make a career, if you are going to write novel after novel until one sticks, be that writer.

These are all things you have to define for yourself, and if you're thinking too much about how other people do it, you will cause yourself no end of pain and you will end up writing less than you could otherwise, or not at all. No one does it exactly the same way. It is the most personal thing in the world that does not involve nudity—or it doesn't for me, anyway, no judgment intended.

Which is why handing out writing advice is a little absurd. It always is because some of it is just basics (Hey, if you're going to write, you need to *read)*, some of it is favorite grammatical fetishes (Banish all passive voice!) and some of it is just how you do (Write naked), and none of it applies to anybody the way it does to you, even if they accept it and it helps them. They're going to make it their own, just like you did when you picked it up wherever you did.

You haven't really advised them, not the way you would, say, if you were a journeyman electrician and an apprentice asked about wire gauge. There aren't any tables of part numbers or standards, here. The audience hears and interprets and holds on to parts of what you say and discards others, which is what happens with your writing, anyway. So many writers love to give advice; it's like writing and publishing a story, only often featuring quicker feedback from a select and captive audience. It feels good, too, to share what you've learned, especially if you might help someone.

Around the same time I stopped writing, I also stopped reading Stephen King. *IT* disappointed me greatly at the time, to put it mildly, and I'd moved on to other writers and genres. I tried to read *The Tommyknockers* and gave up and that was it for King for a long while. I still loved the old books and the Bachman books and almost always loved the short stories as they emerged, but after that, almost every time I read one of King's new novels it was a disappointing experience. My disappointment turned cruel, like old loves can, and I became a rather gleeful critic of King in the occasional published piece and with friends, online and in real life.

And then I read *Lisey's Story*. Or tried to. I gave up, a little infuriated, actually. Boy, did I hate that book. I hated the bad-gunky baby talk and the usual cultural references and references to other King fiction and the magic world and I didn't care about her sisters and…what can I say, I hated the book. I snarked at it in my blog, I think, and a much better writer than me who likes King very much debated my assessment and said that she'd seen a lot that struck her deeply about marriages in it, and she was married and I was not and the conversation pretty much ended there.

Something happened over the next few years: my girlfriend became the woman I wanted to marry. And in talking to friends about this, occasionally, or talking to them about their relationships or reading other people writing about their relationships, the same kind of references would come up to *Lisey's Story*. So I picked the book up again last year and read it again, all the way through. And I loved it. It was all still there, what seemed cloying and cute before, but it didn't now. They were all totally right. How could I have been so wrong?

After that, I started rereading some of the later novels I hadn't liked, and some of them I still didn't like, but some of them I was decreasingly surprised to find I did. Something had changed. I had changed. And I kept reading and eventually, even though I remained fairly critical in public of King, I had to admit that privately I had become a Stephen King fan again. I had lost the indie rocker "Oh, yeah, I like *old* country" excuse. I didn't just like old Stephen King, back when he was good, I liked him now. This was kind of a shock.

Our lives give the best advice, always, not our words. This is not meant to demean words, obviously; you are reading a book of writing advice, after all. But words are ephemeral, and collections of them like this one and every other are in some sense a portable ossuary or, better, insect collection. Here you are, reading what I intended to say a year ago or more, dried and pinned to these pages. Right now, here, as I type, this is all I want to say, the most important thing in the world for me, the single focus of my attention. For you, these words are like light from a star that died ten million years ago. I will certainly not be as focused on this subject when I am done with the article. I will probably not be thinking about it much, if at all, next week. While you are reading this, it is possible that I will not *be*.

Words, the ones that hurt worst, the ones that enrage, the ones that make us laugh, they race so quickly through our lives, and we are acceptably and unacceptably dishonest with them sometimes and some people make a regular habit of that sort of thing. People say things they don't mean for all kinds of reasons, they make unfortunate errors, and they change their minds. If you were godlike and kept cameras on your best friends for ten years straight, you'd see some of them saying precisely the opposite on all sorts of topics as they did once, and then changing their minds again, even. Words matter a lot, but they don't matter like actions. And neither matters like the collection of all actions and words, a life, the biggest story anybody ever tells and the best advice you can ever give, if you do it right.

Stephen King, over the years, has dispensed his share of writing advice publicly, in interviews and a couple of books, in some of his *Entertainment Weekly* columns. He has his basics (You can't watch as much TV as you are right now if you're going to be a writer), his grammar fetishes (Destroy all adverbs!) and the stuff that works for him (Outlining crushes the soul). You will find some of it useful, some of it not, like any other advice. But King has much better advice than that to offer.

Our words can turn out to be empty brag or outright lies, and our lives can tell a different story. Our advice can be useless or even harmful, but the anthology of our actions gives greater wisdom. Our deeds are not static like words, not pictures of events light years away and too many years ago to imagine. What we do, for ill or good, rings out loud and long.

It doesn't matter that Stephen King never really wrote every day from eight to five, stopping only for lunch and two mandatory fifteen-minute breaks. He's written and published more than the rest of us are likely to even start. He is clearly not slacking. This is a piece of advice King never needs speak: *write.* Keep writing. When you stop, when you get lazy or discouraged or a freaking van runs you off the road and you announce to the world you can't do this anymore, start again. Do it anyway.

The following are my favorite pieces of writing advice from Stephen King. I don't think I've ever seen them written down anywhere. I read them in the man himself.

* * *

Your trade is in words. Use them wisely, when you can. Be humble. Be kind. Be gracious. Be generous. Be these things as often as you can. When you are occasionally loud or wrong or acting out some kind of trauma or bad day in front of people, these things will be remembered and you will not be despised.

* * *

Admit it when you're wrong, even if it takes you twenty years.

* * *

Bleed on the page. Put it all down there, go where you go and trust yourself, even if it means ending a novel with a bunch of kids having sex in a sewer to defeat a space spider.

* * *

There is no such thing as too many popular music references.

* * *

Do everything, anything that gets offered to you and sounds cool.

If somebody wants you to direct an Emilio Estevez movie about killer trucks and you've never directed a movie before, do that thing.

* * *

None of this matters more than your wife and kids.

* * *

You can suck it up and shake off *anything*.

* * *

Change your mind.

These are my favorites, the ones I think about, the ones I read in Stephen King's life. Obviously, your mileage may vary.

I forgot your glory, father
I lost your riches to wretches
Now, dry and wasted, I cry
Merciful father
Take me on as a day laborer

- based on the Kontakion of the Prodigal Son, Tone 3

CHAPTER 28

Brian Yount

Banging Our Heads on Padded Walls! Ten Submission Flaws That Drive Editors Nuts.

BRIAN YOUNT is the publisher of *Doorways Magazine,* a quarterly journal of horror and the paranormal. For more information, visit www.doorwayspublications.com.

The editors and I at *Doorways Magazine* have read through thousands of submissions. At times it makes us want to run to the nearest padded room and bang our head. Or sit in the corner, rocking back and forth until the madness of the submission flaws fade away. Why? Because, we see the same errors over and over. It's like listening to a scratched CD that gets stuck on a certain part of a song, and it doesn't take long before the repeating tune drives you insane. The good thing about a scratched CD is you can turn the player off and the problem is fixed. With the submissions errors, there are no *off* buttons. So we decided to offer the top ten flaws that drive us insane, which we hope will eventually serve as a bad submissions *off* button.

1. - Too much telling. This creates a story that is more about the teller, than the tale.

2. - Going overboard with figurative language. Don't use it because you think it sounds good; have valid reasons for implementing.

3. - Cliché situations. Good editors will hardly ever go for a story with an ending that depends on a switch in point to create a twist. It's too forced.

4. - Submission format. Submissions that use anything other than 12-point font size and not double-spaced.

5. - Obvious mistakes. These are errors that could have been caught if the writer would have taken the time to read their work aloud. By doing this you can hear the errors your eyes do not catch.

6. - Make sure every word has a direct relation to the plot. You don't need two pages to tell how the protagonist brushes his teeth. Remember, after writing something, go back and cut, cut, cut.

7. - Stories that rely on style. Concentrate on the story. Fancy words can be a way of disguising a bad story. It's kind of like a cake with fancy icing, it looks good, but if the cake is dry inside, it won't taste good.

8. - Stories with forced dialogue. If your story is strong, but your dialogue is weak, your story just won't gel like it should.

9. - Overhyped cover letter. Sure you can tell us about some of places you've been published, but don't try to convince us you're the greatest writer ever. The fact is, if we accept your story, it had nothing to do with what you told us in the cover letter . . . It all comes down to your story.

10. - Submissions that are nothing close to what we want. This means two things. The writer ignored the guidelines or has never actually read the magazine. If you're going to submit somewhere it's wise to check out what the publisher wants, or has published before.

Hopefully these words will save my padded room some wear and tear.

THE END

Words About *Writers Workshop of Horror*

"Packing more knowledge and sound advice than four years' worth of college courses… It's focused on the root of your evil, the writing itself." — *Fangoria Magazine*

"A veritable treasure trove of information for aspiring writers straight from the mouths of today's top horror scribes!" — *Rue Morgue*

"Entertaining, informative, and also plain old fun, this book will not only make you want to write more, it will give you the tools to writer better. This should be mandatory reading in creative writing classes." — *Horror World*

"An essential cornerstone for any writers' foundation, be they horror writers or otherwise. The advice contained within isn't limited to the horror genre; it addresses all the basic tenets of the writing craft." — *Shroud Magazine*

"… in the chair, and your fingers are on the keys, it doesn't hurt to have a few good manuals and resources a reach away. *Writers Workshop of Horror* is destined to be one of those invaluable resources." — *Dark Scribe Magazine*

"A unique collection of advice and pointers from genre authors who seem excited about the genre and aim to see others succeed." — *The Horror Fiction Review*

"*Writers Workshop of Horror* is just that, a workshop. It's a collection of disparate advice from writers with a variety of backgrounds and at different stages in their professional careers. Here they share their personal, and sometimes contradictory views of the process. And that's a very good thing. Because at some point you have to become your own best critic, and that usually comes after a long process of holding on to advice which feels correct for what you're trying to do, and letting go of perfectly good advice that just doesn't happen to fit your personal aesthetic. It's a long, frustrating process, but with insights from writers like Clive Barker, Ramsey Campbell, Joe Lansdale, Gary Braunbeck, and Elizabeth Massie, this book will help you get there." — Steve Rasnic Tem

"A wonderful resource for writers, and not just horror writers. Much of the advice transcends genre, because a good story is a good story." — Elizabeth Massie, co-author of *D.D. Murphry, Secret Policeman*

"As a writer myself (and a contributor to this volume), I've read rafts of writing-advice books, and I find this is one of the most well-rounded, practical books around. If you care about your craft, this is a wise investment of not just money but time, from people who have been there. Good luck with your writing!" — Scott Nicholson, author of *The Red Church.*

"From grand masters to rising stars, [*Writers Workshop of Horror*] is a treasury of wisdom you'd be hard pressed to find elsewhere. If the (also fantastic) Horror Writer's Association guidebook, *On Writing Horror*, was your introductory course, consider this one your senior year textbook." — *Gorelets*

"Michael Knost has provided us with advice from masters on the specific areas they are known for in a way that gives a broad view of the field. Not only does this impart the discreet bits of info that you need to improve your writing, but it also helps you to see how convoluted of a beast [writing dark fiction] is." — *HorrorNews.net*

"Although the principle focus is on writing horror stories, the gamut of useable information provided is just as applicable to all other genres including romance, westerns, mysteries, science fiction, general fiction, and even biographies. *Writers Workshop of Horror* is a recommended addition to the professional reference collections of all dedicated authors and small press publishers." — *Midwest Book Review*

"*Writers Workshop of Horrors* is twenty-eight interesting articles compiled by editor-author-columnist Michael Knost on the craft of writing horror. Published authors and novice writers will find appealing and applicable topics that may further inspire them. At the very least, readers of this book will be stimulated to think about how horror tales are constructed, and appreciate the workmanship involved." — *Hellnotes*

"There are a number of books available that, while offering similar advice in terms of mechanics, come nowhere near the personal touches Knost brings to the table with his *Writers Workshop of Horror* … Aspiring authors should keep this book within arm's reach at all times." — *Horror Bound Magazine*

"[*Writers Workshop of Horror*], edited by Michael Knost, includes contributions by a dream-team of nationally known authors and storytellers, many Bram Stoker Award winners." — *Majestic 51 Men's Magazine*

"A treasure trove of insightful and interesting information on the craft of horror fiction and I highly recommend *Writers Workshop of Horror* by Michael Knost." — *ExpertsColumn.com*

"Twenty-three articles and three interviews about writing horror, written by some of the best in the field, and all edited by Michael Knost—what's not to like? Practically everything you might need to know gets covered in one or more articles, from handling fight scenes in a horror setting to adding humor. And Brian Keene will step on your aspiring toes with his article, Time, and How to Make it. Overall, it's one of the best compilations of writing advice you can find, and not just for horror writers." — *Withersin Magazine*

"A must-have handbook for horror writers of all skill levels." — David Kinchen, *Huntingtonnews.net*

"When I'm writing, I usually have three reference books close at hand—a paperback dictionary, Strunk & White's *Elements of Style*, and the *Guinness Book of World Records*. Now I'm adding a fourth. With his *Writers Workshop of Horror*, Michael Knost has put together that rarest of books—a writing guide that actually has something valuable to say about the craft of writing. It doesn't matter if you're a beginner or bestseller, this book will pay back the effort you put into reading it. Highly recommended." — Joe McKinney, author of *Dead City* and *Quarantined*

"I was fascinated by *Writers Workshop of Horror* by the time I'd read the first pre-publication announcements. Now with the book in my hands I find it's even more than I expected—28 chapters, each short enough to be absorbed at a single sitting, but packed with information by men and women at the top of the horror-writing field. A treasure well worth the price of admission." — James Dorr, author of *Escape Clause*

"Accessible essays by good writers on a topic that matters to us. What more could we want?" — Janet Berliner, co-author of *Artifact*

"*Writers Workshop Of Horror* helps eager scary storytellers." — *WOWKTV.com*

"A remarkable book, solely focused on the craft—and chock full of valuable advice. You want to learn how to write well? Read this." — Nate Kenyon, author of *The Bone Factory* and *Sparrow Rock*

"*Writers Workshop of Horror* can help make a writer's scary tales even spookier." — *WSAZ.com*

"No matter what type of fiction you write, the words of wisdom collected in this volume will help you by giving insight into common (and not so common) writing problems. A delightful read just on its own—it's a book I will be referring to many times in the future. This one will live on my shelves for years." — Kat Yares, author of *Kats Tales: Journeys Into the Velvet Darkness*

"It doesn't matter if you're just beginning or you've had books and stories published—every writer needs help sometimes. And this book has something for everyone, whether you're looking for tips on how to improve plotting, grammar, dialog, or suspense. It also has helpful hints and strategies for making your stories stronger. This is one of the few books on writing that I actually keep right on my desk and refer to when I'm working."—J.G. Faherty

"Michael Knost has done an excellent job assembling a group of writers that know what they are talking about. While all of these writers are at the top of their respective games, each is known to be especially skilled in one or more aspects of writing. From Elizabeth Massie's Creating Effective Beginnings, through Jeff Strand's Adding Humor to Your Horror, these chapters are all filled with actionable advice that writer's of every level can benefit from." — R. Scott McCoy, author of *Feast*

"[Michael] Knost has wrangled some of horror fiction's finest authors—picking their brains for your benefit. Heed the wisdom of Elizabeth Massie, Tom Piccirilli, Joe R. Lansdale, Clive Barker and, especially, Ramsey Campbell, another master yielding a priceless gem, called The Height of Fear, to keep near at hand for when you need a reminder of how it should be done." — David T. Wilbanks, co-author of the *Dead Earth* books

"In *Writers Workshop of Horror*, editor Michael Knost gathers a stellar line-up of the genre's top talents who give their thoughts and guidance on every aspect of writing horror. The essays and interviews are so insightful and entertaining that one doesn't even have to be an aspiring writer to appreciate this formidable tome; it's a must-read for anyone who loves horror fiction, readers and writers alike! Bravo, Mr. Knost, and thanks for this wonderful book!" — Scott Bradley, co-editor of *The Book of Lists: Horror*

"There are two indispensable books genre writers need at their desk: Strunk and White's Elements of Style and now Michael Knost's *Writers Workshop of Horror*. Not only has Workshop improved my writing and ability to tell an effective story, as an editor and publisher, it has sharpened my eye on what to look for in a successful story. This is a book no one should be without." — Scott Colbert, co-publisher of Bandersnatch Books

"Knost has assembled a to-die-for faculty—a super-panel of horror's best writers and teachers—and gotten them to share with us what they've learned works. These are tips and lessons I wish I'd had starting out." — Steve Burt, author of *FreeK Camp* (July 2010) and winner of the Bram Stoker, Ray Bradbury, and Benjamin Franklin Awards

"*Writers Workshop of Horror* is an incredibly comprehensive book on writing in the genre. This helpful volume is like an instruction manual for new writers, covering all aspects of writing horror and including some dynamite interviews that give insight into how successful writers work and how they think about their writing. Anyone wanting to learn the ins-and-outs of writing horror fiction can't go wrong with *Writers Workshop of Horror*. This is a book that fits nicely into that ongoing and ever-growing library of how to tackle the most intriguing literary genre: horror!" — Nancy Kilpatrick, author of The *Power of the Blood* series

"*Writer's Workshop of Horror* offers a wide range of advice, theory, and even encouragement for the beginning writer, the old pro, and everyone else in the middle. A fun and provocative how-to book of horror." — Paul Tremblay, author of *The Little Sleep* and *No Sleep till Wonderland*

"*Writers Workshop of Horror* is a concise handbook for writers, a rich, working standout in an age of loving literary memoirs that offer little in the way of concrete advice." — Saundra Mitchell, author of *Shadowed Summer*

"Reading Michael Knost's carefully curried *Writers Workshop of Horror* is like walking into an intellectual wardrobe where you get to try on ideas and inspirations from some of the most brilliant designers of fiction today. A cornerstone for any writer's library." —Thomas Sullivan, Pulitzer Prize Nominated author of *The Water Wolf*

"*Writers Workshop of Horror* is a definitive horror handbook for writers who are serious about perfecting their craft. Editor Michael Knost has assembled an impressive roster of industry veterans eager to help up-and-coming authors navigate the vast, sometimes daunting publishing landscape." — Amy Grech, author *Blanket of White*

"If you implement just half the advice from this book, you'll not only become a better horror writer; you'll become a better writer, period. Editor Michael Knost has tasked himself and his writers with laying out virtually all the ingredients of a compelling story (leaving it to you to bake the cake). The result is a how-to book that's as engaging as the high-caliber fiction its authors want so desperately for you to write. This one deserves a spot on your shelf next to Jane Yolen's *Take Joy*, Stephen King's *On Writing*, and Mort Castle's *Writing Horror*." — Pete Mesling

"Those authors who are either seeking to begin writing in the horror genre or are seeking to hone existing skills will gain valuable insight into their craft by reading the recently released *Writers Workshop of Horror*, expertly edited by author Michael Knost, himself no stranger to the horror genre. In this eminently practical volume, Knost has amassed the combined knowledge, expertise, and experience of over twenty of the finest and most talented authors who are fixtures in the Horror genre. The collected essays, each dealing with a different area, aspect, or potential problem area involved in the writing of horror fiction together comprise an organized, practical storehouse of specialized knowledge that rivals, and even exceeds, many far more costly courses on the writing of horror. This book is the best compendium of information and practical advise for the horror author and/or would-be horror author since Stephen King's *On Writing*, and will actually prove to be of far greater worth for those serious about writing horror fiction. The book also happens to be entertaining enough a read to be a worthy perusal for those who enjoy horror literature, even though their interest falls short of actually seeking to write horror as a primary or secondary career or even a hobby." — Norman L. Rubenstein

"I thought *Writers Workshop of Horror* was going to be another run of the mill book about how to write. Boy, was I wrong. It's a goddamn bible. It's that good." – Shaun Jeffrey, author of *The Kult*

"*Writers Workshop of Horror* is a useful compendium of information for aspiring authors of horror and dark fiction, covering everything from the mundane (submission formatting, common grammatical errors) to the sublime (developing themes and finding meaning in writing). The individual chapters, authored by experienced professionals in the field, offer invaluable tips on improving one's writing and one's chances for success as a writer of horror and dark fiction. I found it a valuable resource, and fun to read besides." — H.F. Gibbard

"Like me, you've probably received lots of come-ons from professionals in the horror field. More often than not, you are asked to spend several hundred dollars to listen to someone with only a modicum of experience, probably someone you've never even heard of, let alone read. Now, what if I told you you could attend a workshop with over 25 of the top professionals in horror, successful writers you both know *and* respect? What if they gave you advice on everything from writing that first sentence to characterization and plotting? Now, suppose you could attend this workshop whenever and wherever you wanted, making your own hours and repeating whatever sessions you found valuable? Just how much would such a "dream conference" be worth? I thought so. Well, forget mortgaging the house and selling your car, Michael Knost has distilled that fantasy into a trade paperback that will cost you less than a date at the Cineplex. And, it's portable!" — Mark Onspaugh

"Writers are often asked where they find their ideas. I've not met a writer who doesn't have a trove of ideas and stories waiting—only problem is changing them from an idea into words on a page. The real challenge isn't in coming up with ideas, but rather how to transcribe them effectively onto the page. *Writers Workshop of Horror* lets you sit beside the top dark storytellers today as they shine a light on just how they attack such a challenge. Whether you are just starting to type up those inspirations, a seasoned pro, or a curious reader wondering how these folks do what they do, *Writers Workshop Of*

Horror will leave you inspired and anxious to find what's waiting just around the corner." — John Palisano

"While it is true that you can't teach talent, it is also true that there are many things obvious to the pro that are not to the beginner. Michael Knost's book is full of useful pointers that will shorten the learning curve." — Bob Booth

"Aspiring writers take heart: Inside the covers of *Writers Workshop of Horror,* edited by Michael Knost, lies the blueprint for any story or novel you'd like to construct. Replete with interviews, formatting tips and sage advice, this might be the only horror how-to you'll ever need. In fact, there is such a plethora of apt, interesting and important material, that even seasoned authors may find themselves thumbing it, not only to enjoy the excellent writing therein, but to check against any scene that doesn't work, a character that is less than arresting or a plot that may be sagging—or any other problem that crops up in the course of storytelling. With advice from some of the very best in our business including Joe R. Lansdale, Gary Braunbeck, Elizabeth Massie, F. Paul Wilson, Rick Hautala, Brian Keen, and too many other pros to even name, this is a book no horror writer should be without." — Lisa Mannetti, Bram Stoker Award Winner, Best First Novel, *The Gentling Box*

"*Writers Workshop of Horror* edited by Michael Knost is the most practical and comprehensive guide to writing fiction I have ever read. Contributors include some of the most successful authors in the genre who explain point by point how to construct powerful stories. Every aspect of fiction writing is covered, including how to handle character, plot, setting, dialogue, point of view, action, theme, voice, style and more, along with informative chapters on time management, manuscript formatting and submissions. *Writers Workshop of Horror* is a roadmap to successful fiction writing, an essential reference aspiring writers will want to keep, not on their shelves, but on their desks for easy access. Filled with useful information, concrete examples, and advice from authors who are the best in their field, *Writers Workshop of Horror* is a treasure." — Shannon Riley, Southern Rose Productions

"Smart, fun, and inspirational, *Writers Workshop of Horror* is filled with thoughtful advice and morsels of wisdom from an array of accomplished authors. Whether you're just starting out or looking to hone your skills, this is an entertaining and educational read." — S.G. Browne, author of *Breathers*

"Reading a writer's how-to book often is a mixed bag—at best—replete with articles from authors who may be authoritative in prose but dry as sandpaper in the classroom. Not so here as Knost has assembled a who's-who buffet of the most talented teachers in the genre. They whisk the aspiring writer away into their specialty and leave them both satiated and chomping at the bit to unleash their newly learned weapons." — David Simms

"Pearls of wisdom from those who know. As a former teacher of English and Creative Writing, I nearly cried tears of joy over Jack Haringa's essay 'The Agnotology of Horror.' That piece alone is worth the price of the book!" — Anne Petty, author of *Thin Line Between, Dragons of Fantasy*, and *Tolkien in the Land of Heroes*

"With contributions by the masters of the horror genre, *Writers Workshop of Horror*, edited by Michael Knost, is full of great advice, not only for the aspiring horror writer, but for writers of any genre. Frightfully good!" — Patrick McGinley, author of *The Boathouse*

"*Writers Workshop of Horror* presents the insight and expertise of masters of the genre, from advice on craft to theme and tone to interviews with notables such as F. Paul Wilson and Clive Barker. Editor Knost's own contribution, a selection of authors' "Aha! Moments," may well provide you with your own epiphany; for me it was Sarah Langan's decision that led to her success—to write exactly what she wanted rather than what she thought she should." — Mark All, author of *Mystic Witch*

"*Writers Workshop of Horror* is an essential how-to collection with endless gasoline for burgeoning writers and plenty of tips for seasoned practitioners." — D. Harlan Wilson, author of *Blankety Blank: A Memoir of Vulgaria* and *Peckinpah: An Ultraviolent Romance*

"Not just an invaluable resource for the writer, but an absolute pleasure for the reader, as the genre's best authors offer revealing insights. Essential!" — David Dunwoody, author of *Empire* and *Dark Entities*

"*Writers Workshop of Horror* contains useful tips and advice from professional writers with interesting interviews with Ramsey Campbell and Tom Piccirilli among others. I particularly found Tim Waggoner's advice for considering a change in plot direction very useful and Jeff Strand's 'adding humour to your horror'. This book will be of interest to those just starting out, and also as a refresher for those already published but wishing to go further in their writing careers." — Tony Mileman

"I don't often think of a writing craft book as a page turner, but *Writers Workshop of Horror* kept me hooked. It's like taking part in the coolest class ever, with the funniest, most honest teachers imaginable." — Chris Marie Green, author of *Break of Dawn, Vampire Babylon, Book Three*

"Part of what makes *Writer's Workshop of Horror* so effective is the number of authors heard from. Because their advice and experience covers a wide spectrum, it gives a fly's-eye perspective of the problems and rewards of writing horror. Even the old hand can learn from this collection." — John Alfred Taylor

"Knost's *Writers Workshop of Horror* is the proverbial cornucopia of advice, instruction, and how-I-do interviews. Appropriate for wanna-be's and published authors, the articles present wide views not only for this genre, but writing style and construction of all types. With the likes of Tom Monteleone (as master of religious horror), Tom Piccirilli (a 20 year veteran and Stoker Award winner for Best Novel), and Ramsey Campbell (who can terrify anyone by strolling them around their block), these 28 odd pieces are the next best thing to watching Harlan Ellison produce in a bookshop window. Read it, reference it as needed, and let the sitzfleish reign!" — Peter Dennis Pautz

"*Writers Workshop of Horror*, edited by Michael Knost, comprises essays by over twenty successful horror authors, including celebrities such as Clive Barker, F. Paul Wilson, and Ramsey Campbell, as well as a few interviews. The articles are presented in logical order, with advice on beginnings, middles, and endings first, followed by thoughts on various elements of fiction such as style, dialogue, setting, theme, and tone. Much of this material would apply to writers in any genre, as would Joe R. Lansdale's essay on "Cross Reading" (enriching one's work by reading in many fields, not only one's chosen genre) and Brian Keene's very useful advice on ways to make time to write regularly. Other essays address topics directly related to the craft of horror, such as the nature of fear and how to blend humor with horror. All the contributions are a pleasure to read and packed with specific examples to flesh out their general principles. Highly recommended for aspiring writers of horror and dark fantasy." — Margaret L. Carter

"Knost's *Writers Workshop of Horror* packs a slew of valuable lessons into one easy-to-read guide, whether you're a horror pro who's penned multiple novels or a zombie impaired first-timer trying to tease your nightmares out of your brain onto the page. Particularly helpful are Lansdale's Cross Reading, Maberry's fight scene How To's, Strand's Adding Humor to Your Horror. Before you spill your guts onto the page, make sure to get a copy of *Writers Workshop of Horror*." — Kelly Jameson, author of *Dead On* and *Shards of Summer*

WOODLAND PRESS, LLC

118 Woodland Drive
Chapmanville, West Virginia 25508
www.woodlandpress.com

DISCLAIMER — This book centers on writing better horror and dark fiction and offers principles related to the writing craft, which may be adaptable to other genres as well. It is not the purpose of this manual to reprint all the information that is otherwise available to writers, authors, and/or publishers, but instead to complement, amplify, and supplement other texts currently in existence. You are urged to read all the available material on the subject, learn as much as possible on writing compelling horror and tailor the information in this title to your individual needs. This specific text should be used only as a general guide—and as advice from successful writers within the genre—but not as the ultimate source of writing and publishing information. The purpose of this manual is to educate and entertain. The editor, authors, and Woodland Press, LLC shall have neither liability nor responsibility to any person or entity with respect to any loss or damage caused, or alleged to have been caused, directly or indirectly, by the information contained in this book. If you do not wish to be bound by the above, you may return this book to the publisher for a full refund.

CPSIA information can be obtained at www.ICGtesting.com
Printed in the USA
LVOW07s0630250816

501751LV00002B/110/P